THE WALL STREET JOURNAL.

COMPLETE PERSONAL FINANCE GUIDEBOOK

THE WALL STREET JOURNAL.

COMPLETE PERSONAL FINANCE GUIDEBOOK

JEFF D. OPDYKE

THREE RIVERS PRESS

NEW YORK

Library of Congress Cataloging-in-Publication Data

Opdyke, Jeff D.
   The Wall Street journal complete personal finance guidebook /
Jeff D. Opdyke.
       p. cm.
1. Finance, Personal.   2. Investments.   I. Title.
HG179.O639 2006
332.024—dc22
2005027642

ISBN-13: 978-0-307-33600-2
ISBN-10: 0-307-33600-X

Printed in the United States of America

Design by Mauna Eichner and Lee Fukui

20 19 18 17 16 15 14 13 12 11

First Edition

CONTENTS

INTRODUCTION

For so many people, personal finance is a fairly constrained universe.

They receive a *paycheck*, which they dutifully deposit into a *bank*, at which they own a *savings* and *checking account,* upon which they draw *money* from an *ATM* to pay for their purchases, or upon which they write *checks* to pay the *bills* racked up whipping out a *credit card* to buy dinners, gasoline, and movie tickets. They unleash their *debit card* at the supermarket, and occasionally they stumble into the netherworld of *mortgages* when buying a house or maybe to *refinance* their home when *interest rates* fall. Some opt for a *home-equity line of credit* or a *home-equity loan* when seeking cash to build a pool, after which they rush to increase their *insurance* coverage to protect their *assets* from the *liability* of the neighbor kid taking a header off the diving board and then suing and wiping out their *net worth.* And once every three months they are reminded of their ties to *Wall Street* and the *stocks, bonds,* or *mutual funds* they own when they receive in the mail their account statements detailing the quarter's activity in their *individual retirement account* or the *401(k) plan* they signed up for at work.

After that, personal finance is little more than a mathematical mystery tour. Who has a clue what the *prime rate* is or why it impacts the cost of the new roadster you want to *lease?* Who cares if the ten-year U.S. Treasury note is headed up or down; what does that have to do with the price of your *mortgage payment?* I can't even get my *bank statement* to reconcile with my checkbook. How am I ever supposed to figure out how to calculate my *net worth?* Zero percent financing or $2,000 cash back—does it really matter?

In so many ways, money courses through just about every conceivable corner of our lives. Yet many of us are intimidated by personal finance because, well, it seems intimidating. It has all those . . . numbers. You have to add and subtract and divide. Who has time for that? And a P/E? Wasn't that a class back in elementary school?

Honestly, personal finance isn't rocket science. If you can make change, you can master your money and the skills necessary to manage it effectively. Sure, there are some aspects of personal finance that can be challenging, such as figuring out the inner workings of a variable annuity. Not to worry, though: Even the pros who sell those things often don't know how they work, and, more important, success with your money generally doesn't require that you always know how the sausage is made.

That's where *The Wall Street Journal. Complete Personal Finance Guidebook* comes in. Consider this guidebook your, well, guide to the mystery of personal finance—the money that impacts the way you live, where you live, what sort of car you drive, the number of times you can dine at your favorite eatery each month, and what you can afford to save today for the many tomorrows you must finance. In truth, a vast number of writers have felled a vast number of trees publishing a vast number of personal finance books that offer brilliant advice. But brilliant doesn't necessarily mean practical. This guidebook starts with the realization that financial practicality is more relevant to families than the best laid financial plan. Sure, it might not be the smartest strategy to use your credit card to pay for consumable items that are better paid for with cash. Yet we recognize that in a modern world, personal finances, like water, flow along paths of least resistance. Electronic commerce is a staple of our lives, and, thus, credit cards have become a necessary evil, if only for their convenience and the financial perks that many offer. If you learn how they work, though, and how they can fit productively into your life, you become a better steward of that limited resource known as money.

As such, inside these pages are the facts you need to know to become a savvier consumer of the rapidly increasing lot of financial services that banks, brokerage firms, insurance companies and, yes, credit-card businesses continually peddle to you and your family. The companion workbook, *The Wall Street Journal. Personal Finance Workbook,* is designed to help you start with the basics—balancing your checkbook and calculating your net worth—and then grow with you as your financial needs and sophistication expand. Look for this icon ✎ throughout this book to find the corresponding section in the *Personal Finance Workbook.*

While you won't close this book ready to manage money professionally, you'll certainly learn the tools necessary to master your own finances . . . or at least understand a bit more about all those financial things people jabber about at cocktail parties.

You might be young, just starting out, and wondering how to effectively budget your meager income while still enjoying your life. Maybe you're in your middle years, beginning to save for a child's coming college costs and wondering about the pros and cons of a Coverdell Education Savings Account, a 529 college savings plan, and two strange beasts called UGMA (Uniform Gifts to Minors Act) and UTMA (Uniform Transfer to Minors Act). Possibly you're approaching the end of your career and colleagues or friends insist you need an *annuity,* but you haven't a clue about the differences between a *variable annuity* or a *fixed annuity* or a *deferred annuity* or an *immediate annuity*—or even an *equity-indexed annuity*—and certainly no idea which, if any, is right for your stage of life. And, then again, just maybe you're retired and now realize that *Social Security* doesn't afford the lifestyle you want. You think you might need a *long-term-care* policy that you can't afford, and you've read about these so-called *reverse mortgages* as a way to finance the purchase; but you're not entirely clear on what either animal really means to you or your heirs.

Whatever the case and whatever your age, the basics of what you need to know about personal finance are waiting inside these pages. In easy-to-digest nuggets, *The Wall Street Journal. Complete Personal Finance Guidebook* steers you through the ever expanding realm of everyday money. It helps you know what you should be doing, what you should be avoiding, and what you can do to make your money do its best to meet your family's financial needs. It will guide you through the essentials—such as developing a *budget*—and help you calculate those big financial decisions that stump so many people: Do I rent or buy? Lease or purchase? How much should I save to reach my retirement goals? And how, precisely, do I figure out how much to withhold from my paycheck on my *W-2* form?

In short, consider this book your cheat sheet to the finances of your life.

And it all begins at your local bank.

CHAPTER 1

BANKING

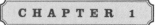

Banks don't come in thirty-one flavors, but numerous varieties exist for what consumers call "banks": nationally and state chartered, commercial, community, federal, merchant, thrifts, savings and loans, building and loans, bank and trusts, credit unions—the list goes on.

Whatever they're called, the basic business of banking is universal: Banks take in your deposits and, in return, pay you some rate of interest. They then turn around and take the very same money you deposited, combine it with deposits from other folks, and lend the money to your neighbor, charging that borrower a higher rate of interest than the bank pays you. The difference between those two interest rates—the so-called spread—is where banks generally make their money.

Businesses deal with commercial banks; consumers deal with retail banks, though in practice many banks service both clients. In 2005 the nation's largest bank was New York–based Citigroup Inc., which provides both commercial and retail banking services and which had total assets of nearly $1.5 trillion. Seattle-based Washington Mutual Inc. was the largest thrift, a consumer operation, with $308 billion in assets, three times larger than its nearest competitor.

Retail banks exist to provide an assortment of products that represent some of the first and most basic personal finance tools for consumers. In the past, savers could stop by just about any local bank and sign up for services that weren't terribly different from the bank down the street. Today, the savviest consumers shop around—both locally and online—since all banks offer different rates and fees for the various savings, lending and credit products they offer. Not every bank peddles the same lineup of products, while others, though they might feature some particular service, aren't trying to make a big business in that arena and, thus, price the service so that it's not particularly attractive to most consumers.

SAVINGS ACCOUNTS

Think back on childhood: A savings account, aside from a piggy bank, was likely your first encounter with real personal finance, and it probably came with a little passbook in which the bank teller recorded your meager deposits. Mom and Dad, maybe your grandparents, opened a savings account for you and stuck a few dollars in there, probably taking the opportunity to tell you about compounding interest, which, at that age, likely generated about as much excitement as Brussels sprouts.

DATE	MEMO	✓	WITH-DRAWALS (−)	DEPOSITS INT. (+)	BALANCE	
3/24	TRANS. FROM checking			2000	15,133	59
					2,000	
1/12	Proceeds stock sale			11,954	17,133	59
					11,954	00
1/12	ATM		300		29,087	59
					300	
1/13	INTEREST (Aug)			16 28	28,787	59
					16	28
1/15	BONUS (3rd quarter)			11,000	28,803	87
					11,000	
1/15	KIDS college ACCT.		60		39,803	87
					60	
1/16	TRANS TO checking		20,000		39,743	87
					20,000	
1/26	ATM		100		19,743	87
					100	00
					19,643	87

Savings accounts are the most basic banking accounts—a place to park your cash and draw interest. Minimum account balances are typically low, sometimes just $5, and the interest rate is equally low, often the lowest among all savings products. But the accounts are FDIC insured and, therefore, "safe"—meaning the full faith and credit of the United States government protects your account against the loss of even a single penny, up to the federal limit of $100,000.

MEMBER FDIC

Look closely and you'll see that just about every advertisement for every bank notes this phrase: "Member FDIC." The initials stand for Federal Deposit Insurance Corp., the federal agency begun on January 1, 1934, as part of President Franklin D. Roosevelt's "New Deal" program to assure depositors burned by thousands of bank failures during the Great Depression that their funds on deposit were fully insured and guaranteed up to $5,000 by the federal government. In other words, with the FDIC the government promised savers who had rushed to banks en masse to withdraw their money that their life savings were safer inside a bank than beneath the mattress or buried in a coffee tin in the backyard.

Today, the FDIC guarantees all deposits up to $100,000 at each bank. That means you can have $100,000 accounts at multiple banks, and each is insured against losses. In fact, a new service has sprung up in recent years called the Certificate of Deposit Account Registry Service, CDARS for short. Banks that participate in this service—there's a list of them at www.cdars.com—offer wealthy clients FDIC protection on as much as $10 million. The banks do this by splitting large deposits into numerous sub-$100,000 accounts that they place at a variety of other banks within the CDARS network. Thus, all the cash falls within FDIC limits.

Insuring more than $100,000 at a single bank is also possible as long as the money is maintained in a different category of legal ownership, such as an individual account and a joint account.

Since its founding, the FDIC has returned to depositors every last penny of insured cash—though some depositors have lost money in excess of the insured coverage.

Savings accounts, in their various forms, are where you want to park money if you expect to need it relatively soon— like when buying a house—or when you cannot afford to risk losing any of the cash.

THE RULE OF 72

"The most powerful force in the universe is compound interest." That comes from Albert Einstein. And he was right as far it relates to money. Consider: The 60 guilders the Dutch paid to buy the New York island of Manhattan in 1626 would, by 2005, have grown to more than 6.4 billion guilders had it been invested at a modest 5% a year and never touched.

Certainly, no one is investing for 379 years, but the point is valid no matter the time span: Compounding's exponential growth means your money works exceptionally hard for you since the interest you earn also earns interest, which in turn earns its own interest—the most pleasant benevolent spiral.

Enter the Rule of 72. Divide 72 by any interest rate, and that's how many years you'll need to double your money. With a 6% rate, for instance, you'll need twelve years to double your account (72 ÷ 6 = 12). Get a 15% return, and your money doubles in about five years (72 ÷ 15 = 4.8).

Aside from the basic passbook account—yes, old-fashioned as they are they still exist at some banks—other types of savings accounts include certificates of deposit and money-market accounts; more on both of these in a moment. Typically, the best interest rates are found online by searching Web sites such as www.bankrate.com.

MONEY-MARKET ACCOUNTS

Think of these as savings accounts on mild steroids. Your money is invested in what is literally known as the "money market"—a vast market of ultra-short-term, highly rated debt obligations issued by various government agencies, corporations, and financial institutions that trade among large institutional investors in very large quantities. Basically, these are IOUs that come due usually within a year, and often within a few weeks

A diversity of banking institutions

or a few months. Because these pieces of paper are highly rated by various credit-rating agencies, such as Standard & Poor's and Moody's Investors Service, the debt is considered safe, meaning there is a negligible risk that the bonds will not be repaid.

Money-market accounts are FDIC protected and pay slightly higher interest rates than standard savings accounts, but the rate is still relatively low. Minimum balances, however, are often relatively high—$2,500 or more. And if the monthly balance slips below that, you'll typically pay a service charge— usually around $10 or so—for every month the account stays below the minimum.

Again, some of the best rates are found online rather than at your local bank. A good resource is www.banx.com. You'll have to register, but it's free, and you'll gain access to a broad listing of banks offering the best rates.

But a warning: While you can deposit money into these accounts as often as you like, withdrawals are usually limited to no more than three to six per month. And because many money-market accounts come with check-writing privileges, a trait not usually associated with a savings product, it's easy to just start writing checks on this account when you need the cash. Banks will cut you some slack the first time you exceed the limit, but beyond that they'll start imposing fees for each transaction over the limit. And if the breaches are persistent, a bank can unilaterally close your account, cutting you a check for whatever balance you have minus any fees the bank might impose. First, though, they'll often send a warning letter. A better approach is to withdraw the money in person or go online and transfer the cash from your money-market account to your savings; those types of withdrawals usually don't count toward the monthly maximum.

Don't confuse money-market accounts with money-market mutual funds. Though related, these two are very different, but more on that later in the Investing section.

CERTIFICATES OF DEPOSIT

CDs, as certificates of deposit are commonly called, are time deposits. That is, you deposit your money with a bank and promise not to touch the cash for a certain period of time. In return for that promise, the bank gives you what are usually the best interest rates it offers on savings products. Banks do this because they know you won't demand this money for several months to several years, which gives them a chance to lend the money and earn a bit of profit on your deposit.

CDs generally span uniform periods of time: three months, six months, nine months, one year, two years, and five years. In practice, there are a variety of other contract periods as well, such as 2½ years, three years, seven years, and ten, among others. When the period ends, a CD is said to have "matured."

Three-month CDs carry the lowest rates, often only marginally better than a money-market account. That's because the bank doesn't have a lot of time to make money off your deposit and must invest it only for the short term. Five-year CDs provide far better rates, usually several percentage points higher than savings accounts, because banks have a much longer period to earn money from your cash.

But don't dive into longer term CDs just to chase a high interest rate. CDs generally impose early withdrawal penalties

INTEREST RATES, APRIL 2005

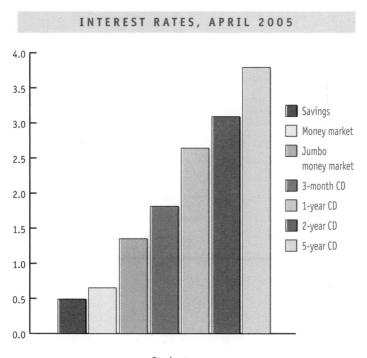

Savings
Money market
Jumbo money market
3-month CD
1-year CD
2-year CD
5-year CD

Bankrate.com

if you reclaim your money before the contract's stated time period expires. The penalties vary, but you typically lose a meaningful amount of interest that has already accrued in your account. So carefully evaluate your near-term cash needs before opting to lock up your money for a long period. Long-term CDs can be a fine way to boost the overall return on your money, but not if you ultimately think there is a chance you might need to break the contract before the CD matures.

One caveat: In some situations, investing in a longer-term CD instead of a short-term contract can be a savvy choice even if you break the CD before it matures. The long-term rate may be high enough and the penalty small enough that the overall interest you receive exceeds what you otherwise would have earned in the shorter-term certificate. Banks aren't going to advertise that, so it's up to you to do the math. ✎ *page 42*

CHECKING ACCOUNTS

"I can't be out of money. I still have checks." That has been a popular bumper sticker for years, and it points to the ubiquity of checking accounts, the cornerstone of personal finance whether it's your own individual checking account or a joint account with a spouse, a partner, or even a parent.

Checking accounts are known as demand-deposit accounts because account holders—those who own a checkbook—can write a check that gives the person you paid the right to "demand" money from your account upon presenting that check to your bank. In the early days of check-writing, that is exactly what folks did; they'd show up at a particular bank in town with a chit signed by a customer of that bank and demand cash in return.

Of course, these days the pizza parlor owner to whom you wrote a check for $19.36 for a large thin-crust with pepperoni and pineapple doesn't need to appear physically at your bank to claim the money. The owner just deposits your check at her own bank, and dozens more like it, all drawn on different banks—some local, some out of town—and all the money she's due ends up in her account within days. This happens because checks carry a variety of oddly rectilinear numbers along the bottom that serve as a bread crumb trail of sorts to help each check find its way home through the national banking system.

The nine digits farthest to the left are the ABA routing numbers that specify which branch of what particular banking company this check is drawn on. The sequence of numbers farthest to the right is the account number, signifying whose account at that branch is to be debited.

Regular checking accounts generally pay no interest. Checking accounts known as negotiable order of withdrawal accounts, or NOW accounts, often do pay interest. But NOW accounts frequently, though not always, require higher minimum balances or charge higher fees than a regular checking

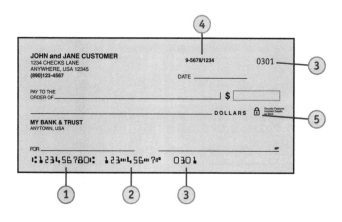

1. **ABA Routing Number:** This nine-digit number is your check's road map through the federal banking system. The number is unique to the bank branch you use, so if you live in Pierre Part, Louisiana, and you send a check to a retailer in Penobscot, Maine, the banks involved know how to route your check back to your bank and, ultimately, your account.

2. **Account Number:** Your unique account number at your bank.
3. **Check Number**
4. **Fraction:** A number that identifies your bank.
5. **Padlock Icon:** An indication that your check has security features incorporated into it to help banks detect fraud. The features are detailed on the back of your check.

account. Some of the best rates and lowest fees on checking accounts are found at credit unions; because they are owned by the members and are nonprofit, credit unions are not consumed with generating fat profits like other banks are.

Whether you bank at a savings and loan, a building society, or a credit union, you'll need to balance your checkbook occasionally—a chore so wretched for many people that they just estimate what they have and then hope for the best. That is an unhealthy approach to your money. You risk being overdrawn, for which the bank will impose a charge of about $25 (roughly the national average for a bounced-check fee), an unnecessary drain on your finances. Or you may risk not knowing you have more money than you realize, leaving you feeling needlessly strapped financially.

A laissez-faire approach to your most basic financial account can also lead to much larger problems with spending and debt since lackadaisical record keeping reflects poor financial management habits. If you can begin to track your checkbook accurately, you'll gain a better grasp on your spending since you'll be more aware of how the debit-card purchases, ATM transactions, and checks you write are really impacting your finances. If nothing else, balance your checkbook to save money. Banks, like humans, aren't infallible; they make mistakes, too, and you want to catch those mistakes in the event they erroneously reduce your account balance.

Of course, if you just can't muster the effort, invest in an inexpensive computerized money-management program such as Microsoft Money or Intuit Quicken. With minimal effort on your part, it will keep the debits and credits in your checking account in a healthy balance. ✎ *page 38*

ATM CARDS

Automated Teller Machines revolutionized banking by allowing customers to interact with their checking and savings accounts absent a bank teller. Stick your plastic magnetized card in the machine, punch in a personal identification number, or PIN, and out comes a wad of cash. As recently as the late 1990s some residents in remote parts of Alaska refused to deal with ATMs, considering them devil machines because they couldn't understand how or why it would dispense money.

Banks love ATMs because they dramatically cut demand on tellers, thereby saving money. And by charging non-bank customers a fee of between $1 and $4 per transaction to use the machine, ATMs generate lots of noninterest income. That surcharge might seem a small price for convenience, but hit an ATM not affiliated with your bank once a week for a year, and you've spent as much as $200 just to access your own money—and that doesn't count the $1 or more your own bank will levy each time you venture outside your bank's own ATM network.

Thus, if you're a frequent ATM user, it is best to look for a bank with lots of convenient ATM locations, including those inside nearby supermarkets, where banks are increasingly locating mini-branches. Banks typically list ATM and branch locations on their Web sites. Also, check for banks that have surcharge-free ATM machines.

If you can't find an ATM for your bank, then use a competing bank because the fee is usually lower than you'll find at independently owned machines inside gas stations, hotels, casinos, and convenience stores.

By the way, the blandly named Electronic Fund Transfer Act limits your loss to $50 if your ATM card is stolen and cash is ultimately siphoned from your account. But you must report the card lost within two days of noticing its disappearance. Wait longer and your liability rises significantly.

DEBIT CARDS

Don't feel like searching out an ATM or don't want to pay the fee to use one outside your bank's network? That's where debit cards come in. They look identical to credit cards (and some serve that function as well), but they act more like ATM cards (and some serve that function, too). Instead of taking on debt as you would when buying the week's groceries with a credit card, you are instead, with the swipe of your card through the electronic reader, authorizing the grocer to directly withdraw funds from your bank account, usually a checking account.

This is an immediate transfer, exactly as though you pulled the money from your account at the ATM. That means you cannot float a purchase until the credit-card bill arrives. If you don't have enough money in your account, your transaction won't go through.

Debit cards are increasingly popular among consumers and retailers since the cards act like electronic cash. For the consumer there is no need to carry money or checks, yet you don't accumulate interest charges as you do when paying for purchases with a credit card. That allows for better financial management because you see immediately the effect that even a single small purchase has on your checkbook balance and your monthly spending and savings goals. With a credit card the effect of all but the largest, most memorable purchases are lost in the fog of all the random spending you do each month. And because most debit cards are accepted globally—generally anywhere major credit cards are taken—you don't need to pack nearly as many traveler's checks or as much cash as you ordinarily would.

Retailers love debit cards because the cash transaction is instantaneous and there's no need to pay the fees that credit-card companies impose on merchants for each purchase. Beware, though: Some merchants impose their own fee on consumers paying with a debit card. So ask before swiping.

ONLINE BANKING

With the advent of the Internet, online banking has surged in popularity and has replaced the ATM as the most convenient form of banking. Where else can you download a recent history of your checking account, watch for your paycheck to be directly deposited, shuffle money between various accounts while paying your bills electronically, and apply for a home-equity loan, all at three in the morning, while sitting in your underwear, watching *Bonnie and Clyde,* one of the great bank-heist flicks of all time?

Online banking takes two forms: access to an account that is otherwise held at a bricks-and-mortar branch down the block, and banking with a financial institution based entirely in cyberspace and thus having no physical bank branches.

Either approach essentially offers the same broad cast of options depending on services available at a particular bank. You can transfer money back and forth between various accounts at the bank; reorder checks when you run out; pay various bills electronically; stop payment on a check; apply for

loans, mortgages, and credit cards online; open a CD online and fund it with money from your savings account; find the nearest ATM; order foreign currency for an upcoming Asian vacation; and request a home or auto insurance quote. The list goes on.

Most bricks-and-mortar banks offer online services these days and are eager for customers to partake since whatever you do electronically cuts down on the costly face-to-face time needed for in-person transactions. As for the online-only banks, they have no real infrastructure costs for building, staffing, heating, cooling, securing, and lighting an armada of branches. Because their overhead is so much lower, Internet-based banks generally pay higher interest rates on their savings products and often charge lower fees on their various accounts and loans. Take, for example, EmigrantDirect.com, the online division of New York City–based Emigrant Savings Bank. In mid-2005, Emigrant Direct offered the American Dream Savings Account that paid 3.5% annually on balances as small as $1. By comparison, the national average was a full percentage point lower and at many banks balances as large as $250,000 earned less than 1.5% annually.

Cash in an Internet bank carries the same $100,000 FDIC protection. Typically with Internet banks, you'll have to establish a direct-deposit link or make deposits through certain ATM networks with which a particular Net bank has teamed up. The mail is another option, though the delay makes this approach best suited to an online savings, money-market, or CD account since this is money you don't plan on needing to tap quickly for life's daily expenses.

You can access your money though various ATMs. Most Net banks don't charge you for this, though the bank that owns the ATM very well could. Recognizing that as a hindrance, some Internet banks reimburse a certain number of ATM transactions each month. Online banks also typically provide a list of ATMs that are totally free of charges, though there is no guarantee any of those ATMs are nearby.

THE RIGHT ACCOUNT

It all comes down to this: What bank is right for you?

Well, there's not one kind of bank, so there's not one simple answer. The right bank for you depends entirely on how you bank and what services you demand.

Start by assessing your banking needs. For instance, are you a check writer or an ATM junkie? If you write a lot of checks, you want to find a bank that has an account that allows for unlimited check writing each month without imposing a charge because some accounts levy a per-check fee after you hit a certain volume in a given month. If you rely on the ATM for your cash supply, then search for a bank with an abundance of local machines. You can easily compare fees and services on the Web sites that all banks maintain.

Here are some considerations when choosing an account:

- What are the most convenient times for you to do your banking? If you work odd hours and can't get to the branch during the week, then you might want a bank with Saturday or even Sunday hours—a trend many banks are moving toward these days.

- What is your typical bank balance? If you generally keep a relatively small amount of dollars in your account—say, less than $500—then aim for a basic free checking account that allows for low or no-minimum balances without charging monthly maintenance fees. The downside is that your services will likely be limited, and you probably won't be paid interest on the money sitting in your account, but at least you won't be paying money every month just to keep your dollars safe. On the other hand, if you routinely keep a sizable amount of cash in your account, you'll have more options, including checking accounts that pay interest. Remember, too, that you don't always have to have the big balance in just one account; many banks will aggregate the balances in your various accounts.

BREAKING UP IS EASY TO DO

 You may find one day that you need to close a bank account. Maybe you're moving to another city. Maybe you're getting married and combining accounts at your partner's bank. Maybe you're just tired of paying the fees to keep your account open. Whatever the reason, following these steps will make the process easier.

1. Before you close your old account, open a new account at your chosen bank. This will make it easier to move the money when you go to retrieve the cash from your former bank. If the new bank is in a new city, call up the branch near where you'll live. Tell them you're relocating and you'd like to open a new account. They'll often help you over the phone or will send the requisite documents to you.

2. Balance your checkbook so that you know exactly how much money you should have in the account. This ensures that you don't reclaim all the money the bank thinks you have when you still have several outstanding checks that haven't cleared the system. You don't want to pay any bounced check fees.

3. If you have checks directly deposited into your old account, or if you have automatic debits pulled from your old account—for insurance or investments and the like—notify the appropriate companies weeks in advance of your new account information. The switchover can take several days to a couple of weeks. Also, you want to leave your old account open until you are certain that all automatic transactions are occurring in the new account. That means leaving enough money in the old account to cover any automatic debits in case your instructions don't make it to the right department in time.

4. Make certain that you give your former bank your new contact information, including address and work, home, and mobile numbers. Give the information to your local branch manager and send a letter to the home office as well to make sure the data makes it into the bank's data-

base. This serves two purposes: If new transactions hit your closed account, they'll know how to reach you, and the bank will know where to send your tax forms when tax season arrives.

5. Finally, don't forget about your safe-deposit box if you have one.

※

- Do you bank electronically? If you'd rather bank online instead of waiting on line at the bank, then check out each local bank's Internet services. That way you'll be able to gauge how useful their site is and whether you'll be charged for banking or paying bills electronically since some banks do impose fees depending on the type of account you open. Also, many banks offer free checking or will even rebate your account a couple of dollars each month if you sign up for direct deposit.

- Is a personal relationship important? Maybe you like standing on line to talk to the teller or to physically deposit your paycheck into your account through the drive-up window. If so, be sure the bank or account you choose doesn't charge a fee for each in-person transaction. Some banks and certain types of low-minimum or Internet-only accounts offered by standard bricks-and-mortar banks hit you with a service fee if you use anything other than the ATM to withdraw or deposit money.

In the end it comes down to this: Banks offer the most basic financial accounts, but each bank puts its own spin on what bells and whistles each product features. Thus, it pays to spend a little time researching the various offerings available at the local banks, thrifts, and credit unions in your town. With so many types of banks all competing for retail clients, you're bound to find an account that fits your needs quite well.

CHAPTER 2

BORROWING

Outside of banking, borrowing represents the second most common personal finance transaction that consumers deal with. Think about how often you yank a credit card from your wallet to pay for groceries, gas, haircut, vacation, car rental, or a vet bill. These days you can even pay your taxes with a credit card.

Credit, for all the responsibility it entails, is surprisingly easy to come by. Did you check the mail today? Chances are you have at least one credit-card company—probably more— itching to give you a new card and a line of credit that you can start running up immediately.

In many instances, debt can be a means to a valuable end, particularly when used prudently in pursuit of purchases that hold long-term value, such as an education, a home, or a small business. Even borrowing to buy a car can be wise as long as you are smart about it.

But debt can also tear your life apart. It can destroy friendships and marriages. It can rob you of your retirement savings and cause you to lose your home. It can leave you dependent on the basic income that Social Security provides and leave your spirit crushed. In 2004 more than 1.56 million personal bankruptcy filings were made by an estimated 2.06 million individuals and couples, their lives now altered in many ways.

In short, debt is both benevolent and malevolent. Deciding

which form it takes in your life is entirely up to you. Let's look at how borrowing works and how it can affect your finances.

WHAT IS DEBT?

Debt is a very simple concept: You borrow money you don't have to buy something you otherwise can't afford to pay for now. The purchase might be small, such as a beverage that costs $1 at McDonald's, and you stick it on your credit card because you're out of cash. Or the purchase can be huge, such as a million-dollar beach house for which you take out a thirty-year mortgage.

In either transaction you are the *borrower* and the person or company who lent you the money is the *lender.* The money you borrowed is the *principal,* and you repay it with *interest,* the charge the lender imposes for giving you access to money you otherwise wouldn't have. In repaying the borrowed money you typically have anywhere from one month (with a credit card) to several decades (with a mortgage).

Not all debt is created equal, however. Like cholesterol, some debt is good, some is bad. In managing your finances effectively, your aim is to use the good debt when it is appropriate and avoid bad debt as much as possible.

GOOD DEBT

Good debt improves your life for a long time. That last phrase, *for a long time,* is key. Bad debt can improve your life in the immediacy of the moment, but the usefulness of the purchase often fades quickly, within days if not hours, and ultimately has no residual value.

Good debt includes the following:

- **An affordable home.** Home ownership is the basis of much wealth in the United States, and the home is often the single most valuable asset Americans own. Unless you win the lottery, inherit a sizable sum, or rob a bank and get away with it, chances are you'll need to take on debt via a mortgage to buy a house. We'll get into this more later in this section, but you don't want to buy a home that is ultimately more than you can afford. You could find yourself stressed about the large monthly note, and if you are ever strapped financially, paying that note and the requisite home owner's insurance and property taxes could prove too much. You could ultimately lose your house in a foreclosure when the lender steps in to reclaim property for which you are no longer able to pay.

- **Education.** The value of a college degree can't be overstated. The earning power you attain over a career will far outshine the original cost of the degree even if the cost is $100,000 or more. Yes, it's true that numerous high school dropouts and some people who never went to college ended up very successful, but they can be likened to the infinitesimal sliver of high school athletes who made it into the professional ranks.

- **Rental or investment real estate.** As the old cliché says, "They're not making any more land." Riches have been accrued by landowners for eons, and, historically, real estate has been a sound investment—as long as you're not buying into wildly speculative markets. Using debt to buy a piece of property that someone else will rent from you for more than the cost of your monthly payment is a tried-and-true strategy for accumulating wealth and generating income.

- **A car.** This goes against the conventional wisdom of many professional planners who argue that a car, because it is a depreciating asset, is not a good use of debt. In the abstract that is probably right. But life isn't abstract, and in most cases, a car in modern society is a necessity. It provides an improved standard of living by allowing people access to better schools or better neighborhoods than they would otherwise have access to if they relied solely on mass transit. A car allows you to commute to a better-paying job ill-served by public transit to begin with, and in many cases it makes sense to take out a car loan for the purchase.

BAD DEBT

Basically, if you consume it, if it loses value over time, or if you have to feed it, it's bad debt.

That's the simplistic definition, and it includes meals, vacations, a fill-up at the gas station, groceries, toys for the kids, an afternoon iced latte, a new flat-screen TV for the family room, a new goldfish, flowers for the front yard—essentially all the random consumer detritus we charge to our credit cards every day.

For the most part these are items you should be paying for with cash. The reason is that cash keeps you in tune with your finances. If you start your week with $50 in your wallet and on Monday you spend $17 on lunch, a battery for your watch, and a coffee on the way back to the office, you know you have $33 left for the rest of the week. But when you put those transactions on a credit card, it's like spending Monopoly money: It just doesn't register as real. They are easily forgotten because they're so numerous and relatively small. But over time, even in just a single month, the forgotten $12 here and the $9 there can add up to hundreds or thousands of dollars owed to American Express or MasterCard.

What is worse, if you can't pay the full amount, part of what you owe rolls over to the next month and accumulates interest, increasing your balance. Soon you may find yourself in a vicious cycle in which your income doesn't equal your spending. That load of debt can grow larger and at some point control your life.

But, as noted above, that is the simplistic view. In reality, using a credit card to make some of those purchases isn't in itself bad. Not moderating your spending during the month and not paying your full balance when the credit-card bill arrives is where debt goes bad. So let's take a look at credit cards.

CREDIT CARDS

A credit card is a financial tool that allows you to purchase goods and services when you don't have the necessary cash on hand. Like any tool, a credit card can work productively or destructively.

A credit card can be an efficient way to spend, and in a society that increasingly is going cashless, having one has become a necessity. Just try reserving a car or booking a hotel room without a credit card these days. Of course, a credit card can also be an efficient way to satisfy wants you otherwise can't afford or that are a waste of your limited resources, thereby shriveling your net worth over time. That is the epitome of bad debt.

Here's how it works: A credit-card company fronts you the money for your purchase by promising to pay the retailer or the service provider the cost of whatever you've bought. In return you promise to repay the credit-card company the full amount. If you repay the money in full within thirty days, the credit-card company typically doesn't impose any interest. If you don't repay the entire amount, then interest begins to accrue on the outstanding balance.

If you repay all your balance in full each month, you have effectively gained access to free money. That's because the money you otherwise would have spent on groceries and gas and such is instead sitting in your bank earning interest. That's a wise use of debt. But do read the fine print on your contract; some card companies now charge a fee when you pay your balance in full each month because otherwise they get nothing from you for the use of their cash.

Credit and charge cards come in several varieties, but the big three are American Express, Visa, and MasterCard. Discover and Diner's Club have their followers, but those cards

CHARRRRRRGGGE IT!

"Credit cards" and "charge cards," while used interchangeably by consumers, are not identical. Credit cards extend to you a line of credit, your spending limit, and allow you to carry a balance, for which you are charged some interest rate. Charge cards generally require you to pay your balance in full every month instead of carrying all or a portion of it over to the next month. For that reason, charge cards have no spending limit and no interest rate. You can spend as much as you want each month without fear of bumping up against your spending limit, as long as you pay the balance in full each time the bill arrives.

The most famous charge card is the American Express card, which comes in green, gold, platinum, and black. The green card is the basic card, while the gold and platinum cards come with a variety of extra perks for which you pay a larger annual fee. For instance, with the platinum card (annual fee $350), if you buy a business-class airline ticket for an international flight on one of a handful of major airlines, you can get a companion ticket for free.

The black card, meanwhile, officially known as the American Express Centurion Card, is the most selective—and elusive—piece of financial plastic in the world. Only an estimated five thousand Americans own one. The cost of membership is a $2,500 annual fee and $250,000 in annual spending on an existing AmEx card.

are also-rans at best. Though there are a small number of types of cards, there are literally thousands of iterations floating around, all with different affinity branding on the front and all with different costs, interest rates, fees, and perks. Some cards offer airline miles with which you can obtain free airline tickets or hotel stays, saving potentially thousands of dollars in airfare or vacation costs. Some cards offer rebates, returning money to you at the end of the year or credits for free gas or discounts on a new car. Some cards contribute money to a college savings plan for your children, essentially helping you fund some portion of your future college bill just by spending money on the everyday things you have to buy anyway, such as the week's groceries.

All of those can prove smart uses of debt as long as you're not accumulating interest charges and you're not overspending. The smartest credit-card consumers are those who know they can afford to pay cash for what they're buying but choose to use a credit card for some added benefit they're getting, whether it's free use of the credit-card company's money or airline miles that will whisk them off to the Milford, New Hampshire, Great Pumpkin Festival in the fall.

Consumers go astray when they rely on credit cards to live a lifestyle their income can't support. Maybe you just love the styling of those new Manolo Blahnik pumps, or maybe you're absolutely certain that the new Big Bertha golf club will shave six strokes off your game. But if you can't afford those purchases with the cash in your checking account, then you can't afford those purchases. It's as simple as that.

Prudently using a credit card means paying attention to how much debt you're racking up in charges so that you have enough cash from your monthly income to pay the bill when it arrives. You never want to fall into the habit of routinely drawing down your savings to pay a credit-card bill; in that event all you're doing is consuming your assets through items with no store of value. You can argue that a vacation has value because it revitalizes you. But if

GOOD VERSUS EVIL

If you could pay cash for what you want and are certain you'll pay the credit card in full each month, but you're using a card for a perk that ultimately improves your finances, then the debt is likely benign. If you can't pay cash for what you want even if you raid your checking account, and you know you'll have to carry a balance on your card for a couple of months to repay the purchase, then the debt is malevolent and your finances will suffer over time.

it means you can't save money or contribute to a retirement plan, you'll never be able to trade memories of that week in Waukesha for the peanut butter and Tender Vittles you'll need to live on in retirement.

To keep track of your monthly spending, set aside a basket, a drawer, a bowl, or whatever works best for you, and toss into it every receipt you accumulate each day. Keep a running tally of the charges on a piece of paper. You'll see exactly how much you're on the hook for, a visual reminder that will likely keep you from overspending. This serves a security purpose as well. If your bill shows you owe more than your tally says you owe, you either forgot to record an expense or someone has fraudulently tapped into your account, and by quickly noticing the added charge, you can alert the credit-card company to the nefarious activity.

Equally convenient is routinely visiting your credit-card company's Web site; most likely it is printed on the back of your card and certainly it is on the monthly statement. You can see exactly how much you owe at any given moment, though your most recent charges might not be in the system yet.

Remember this: When it comes to debt, particularly from a credit card, it's your spending, not your income, that ultimately determines your wealth. You can save all you want, but if you have an untamed credit-card habit, all that money—and more—will wind up on the profit line of your neighborly credit-card company.

HOW MUCH IS TOO MUCH DEBT?

Let's concentrate on bad debt here. We'll discuss good-debt levels later in relation to buying a home.

In short, you're bumping up against the bounds of prudence when your bad-debt load hits 20% of your take-home pay—and something near 15% is more conservative. That means if you bring home $40,000 a year after taxes, your bad debt shouldn't exceed a cumulative $8,000, or $6,000 if you're

WHEN MINIMUMS MEAN MAXIMUM PAIN

It looks so easy. Just pay the minimum payment printed on the credit-card bill each month, and all is well. You stay in the good graces of your credit-card company, you're paying down your debt, and you can continue to use your card for important missions to the mall.

The average American consumer carries roughly $8,562 in credit-card debt. Bankrate.com reports as of April 2005 that the average fixed-rate credit card charges an interest rate of 11.82%. Many cards require minimum monthly payments equal to 2% of the balance. Now, let's assume you are this average credit-card customer, and you never charge another item on this card. How long will it take you to repay your debt making just the minimum monthly payments? And, equally important, how much will it cost you?

Astoundingly, you'll need twenty-nine years to fully repay the debt. And over that time you will pay an additional $8,016 in interest charges, essentially doubling your bill. For the privilege of amassing more than $8,500 on dinners and movies and vacations that you didn't have the cash to pay for in the first place, you now have three decades to reflect on all the joy those expenses brought you—that is, of course, if you can recall that sushi dinner twenty-nine years ago.

In short, always pay more than the minimum.

⁂

playing by the 15% rate. That figure includes your credit-card debt as well as several other potentially bad-debt accounts:

- **A home-equity loan or outstanding balance on a home-equity line of credit.** While a first mortgage is creating value through home ownership, home owners often sign on for home-equity loans and lines of credit to meet consumer spending wants. This is bad debt.

- **Affinity charge cards with a balance.** You go into the Gap for a pair of pants and a shirt, and the clerk offers you a 10% discount today if you sign up for the Gap's in-house credit card. Hey, you're saving money. Wise consumer decision, right? Not even close. You are accumulating more debt for a consumable and are compartmentalizing it on yet another card. Later in the month you'll check your Visa bill online and be happy to see you owe only $35. You'll have forgotten about the $500 you racked up on cards from the Gap, Nordstrom, Pottery Barn, and Home Depot. Plus, you're impacting your credit score (more on that momentarily). And woe be to those who sign up for a store credit card that lets them delay payments on pricey items such as electronics or furniture until sometime after the next lunar eclipse. Bad, bad debt all around.

- **Auto leases and car notes.** Yes, this contradicts the comments above about car debt not necessarily being bad debt. Nevertheless, in terms of calculating your debt load you must include them here. A modest-rate loan on a modestly priced car note isn't necessarily bad, but an auto lease must certainly be included. With a car you own outright, even though it depreciates in value, there is still typically a residual value in the asset once the loan is repaid. With a car lease, at the end of the lease term you turn the car back in and receive no money. Or you must come up with the cash to cover the residual value. Moreover, leases are often the playground of drivers who demand more car than they rightfully should be buying. This is most assuredly bad debt.

To calculate your debt-to-income ratio, tally your total annual debt payments for all your bad debt. Then divide that number by your annual income. The resulting number represents the level of debt you're carrying. Sticking with the $40,000 income, assume you have a monthly car lease of $350, a store charge card on which you're paying $25 a month, three credit cards with combined minimum monthly payments of $112, and a home-equity line of credit you took out to pay for a vacation on which you now pay $300 a month. Your total monthly obligation is $787, or $9,444 a year—the equivalent of 23.6 percent of your take-home pay. Too much bad debt. ✎ *page 64*

The ideal amount of bad debt (isn't it obvious?): zero.

WHERE TO FIND THE BEST CREDIT CARD

That depends entirely on how you use credit.

If you pay off your balance every month and rarely let it carry over, you'll do well with a card that imposes no annual fees and doesn't charge you for paying your balance in full. If you carry a balance from month to month, however, you want a low-interest-rate card so that your monthly interest charges are as small as possible. That will free up more money in your spending plan to pay down your debt sooner.

To find a more consumer-friendly card, check out www.bankrate.com or www.cardweb.com. Both provide regularly updated information on low-rate cards for consumers who typically carry a balance as well as those who pay off their balance monthly. By way of example, in the spring of 2005, Pulaski Bank offered a no-fee gold MasterCard with a fixed interest rate of 6.5%. Beware of promotional rates, however. Alongside the Pulaski card was this offering: the Chase Speedway SuperAmerica Platinum card with a promotional rate of 0.0%, but it later jumped to 20.24%.

CREDIT REPORTS AND CREDIT SCORES

It used to be that our Social Security number defined us. These days it is increasingly our credit report and credit score. Not only are they used for the obvious purchases—a new house, a new car—but TXU Energy in Texas in 2004 floated the idea of using credit scores to determine utility rates charged to certain customers, imposing higher rates on customers who had previously fallen behind on telephone, power, or cable TV bills. The energy company temporarily suspended the plan after receiving much grief from regulators and consumer advocates.

Nevertheless, that episode shows how pervasive reliance on credit scoring has become. For that reason it is imperative that consumers not only strive to maintain a respectable credit history but be vigilant in ensuring that their credit reports and credit scores accurately reflect that history. One wrong entry can take money out of your pocket when lenders charge you higher interest rates—or utility companies charge you higher rates—simply because your credit score is lower than it should be.

Credit reports are provided by one of three companies: Equifax, Experian, and TransUnion. Though they all do the same thing, the information they have isn't necessarily identical. One might show a payment delinquency, for instance, that the other two don't.

Credit scores are provided by Fair Isaac Corp. in the form of your FICO score. That score is based on the information in your credit reports and is calculated based on a proprietary mathematical formula. It defines you in terms of the credit risk you represent to a lender.

Every time you apply for credit, be it a home loan or a Circuit City credit card when you purchase a surround sound speaker system, lenders buy a credit report and examine your credit score to determine how worthy a borrower you are. The higher your score, the lower the risk you are. Conversely, the lower your score, the greater risk the lender assumes. To compensate for the risk that you ultimately won't make good on your obligation to pay for the surround sound system, the lender jacks up the interest rate it charges you. So the lower your score, the more you ultimately pay.

The biggest reason credit scores are so important is that they determine how much money you must shell out every month for your purchases. That's because lenders set different rates for borrowers in different credit-score ranges.

Let's say you want to buy a new car, and the loan is $15,000. You want to pay it over forty-eight months. Here, courtesy of the Loan Savings Calculation at www.myfico.com, are the different rates that lenders might charge in mid-2005, based on different credit scores, and how that affects your monthly note:

FICO Score	APR (Percent)	Monthly Payment ($)	Total Interest Paid ($)
720–850	5.745	351	1,825
690–719	6.517	356	2,080
660–689	8.544	370	2,762
625–659	10.712	386	3,508
590–624	14.448	413	4,837
500–589	13.018	403	4,322

Bad credit has a very real impact. In this example it can mean you pay as much as $3,000 more than your neighbor with good credit for the exact same car.

WHAT'S A GOOD CREDIT SCORE?

FICO scores run from a low of 300 to a high of 850. The median score in the United States was 723 in mid-2005, and the largest group of consumers—28%—were in the 750 to 799 range.

But what defines "good" is often a blurry matter. There is no single industry-wide definition of good because different lenders look differently at different scores—and even that can change from one day to the next depending on the type of business a particular lender is looking to attract.

WHERE TO GET YOUR CREDIT REPORT AND CREDIT SCORE

The three credit-reporting agencies and Fair Isaac will gladly sell you a copy of your credit report and your credit score anytime you'd like one. All of them also provide services, for which they charge various fees, that allow you to monitor changes to your credit report during the year and that give you access to your credit score. This can be a particularly handy service for thwarting identity theft if ever you lose your wallet. The agencies will alert you to any requests for new credit that pop up in your name. These are their Web sites:

www.equifax.com

www.experian.com

www.transunion.com

www.myfico.com

You can also obtain a free copy of your credit report annually. A 2004 change to the Fair Credit Reporting Act requires the credit-reporting agencies to provide you with a free copy of your credit report every twelve months. Order the reports at www.annualcreditreport.com or call 877-322-8228.

Also, if you are ever denied credit based on what was contained in your credit report, you are entitled to a free copy of your report so that you can see why a lender has deemed you unworthy. The lender that denied you credit must give you the name, address, and telephone number of the credit-reporting agency that supplied the report, and if you contact that agency within sixty days, it must provide you with a report for free.

FIXING ERRORS

Here is a disheartening statistic: A 2004 research report found that 25% of all credit reports contain errors serious enough to cause consumers to be denied credit, a loan, an apartment, and even a job. That's reason enough to scour every inch of every credit report you're entitled to.

Check them all because although the agencies are collecting very similar data, one error at one credit agency, even if it doesn't show up at the other two, can dent your credit worthiness.

How, though, do you deal with the bureaucracy of erasing the errors on your credit report?

Start by gathering whatever documentation you can to prove your claim. Contact the lender that dinged your credit; you're seeking information on the source of the disputed charge. It could be something as simple as a typo in a Social Security number, or maybe you're John J. Smith and the lender meant to blackball John K. Smith (the letters are next to each other on the keyboard). Recognize that this is just to help you prove your case to the credit-reporting agency. The lender has no obligation to tell the credit-reporting agency to fix something, though some may well do that for you.

However, the credit-reporting agency *does* have an obligation under the Fair Credit Reporting Act to correct errors. So this is where you should concentrate your efforts. Alert the credit-reporting agency of the error. You can dispute the error online with the three credit-reporting agencies, or in writing. If you do so in writing, send the letter by certified mail so that you can prove it arrived in case the agency plays

CREDIT-REPORTING AGENCIES

Equifax Information Services
P.O. Box 740256
Atlanta, GA 30374

Experian
P.O. Box 2002
Allen, TX 75013

TransUnion
P.O. Box 1000
Chester, PA 19022

dumb or if your dispute ends up in court. By law the agencies have just thirty days to respond to your request to fix the error and must notify other agencies of the correction if an error mars your report. Also, the Federal Consumer Information Commission, those good folks in Pueblo, Colorado, have a sample dispute letter that you can crib from their Web site, www.pueblo.gsa.gov.

Assiduously keep records of all correspondence. That means printing your original online dispute. Also ask for the full name of anyone you talk to on the phone as well as the supervisor's name, since you never know when call-center workers will move on to other jobs. Keep copies of all letters and documents you send and receive from the original creditor and the credit-reporting agency.

If the error is not corrected and you are confident it is wrong, then you should contact a lawyer and present all your evidence. Let the lawyer take it from there.

IMPROVING YOUR CREDIT

As an Eddie Murphy character, paraphrasing Nietzsche, said in the movie *Coming to America,* "One cannot fly into flying." That's applicable to repairing the blemishes on your report that aren't errors. Those blemishes take time to repair. Basically, there's no quick way to fly.

Those dings stick around for seven years—ten years if you have filed for bankruptcy. But you can take some action to begin improving your report and your credit score.

- Begin paying your bills consistently on time. A late payment in recent months can hurt your score more than a late payment several years back.

- Reduce your outstanding balance. The amount of money you currently owe in relation to the credit available to you weighs heavily on your credit score.

- Pay off your debt rather than shift it onto other cards. This seems quirky, but if you have $2,000 spread across five cards currently, realigning that balance onto just two cards and then closing the other three could actually lower your credit score. Here's why: Say the combined credit limit of those five cards is $10,000. Your balance represents 20% of your available credit. But if you cancel three, and this means your combined credit falls to $5,000, your balance now represents 40% of your available credit. This relatively high number can hurt your credit score.

- Never apply for store-branded credit cards just to get the immediate discount. Increasing the amount of available credit lowers your score since it shows lenders that you have the ability to go out and in a fit of binge shopping pile on a ton of debt, which might leave you unable to pay this new debt you're looking to take on.

- Don't apply for new credit cards if you don't need them. The new cards lower the average age of your account, making it appear in FICO calculations that you haven't had credit as long as you really have. That, too, lowers your score.

- Don't cancel your oldest card. This ties in to the comment above. Your first credit card, even if it is now charging you a 40% interest rate, establishes the longest history of credit worthiness in your name. If you cancel the card, you could reduce your credit track record and, as a result, lower your credit score unintentionally. Instead, keep the card someplace safe or even cut it up so that you never use it—but don't call the card company to cancel it.

THE HOME FRONT

For most Americans buying a house is the largest purchase they'll ever make; the price of an average home in the United States was about $250,000 in late 2004. Moreover, they'll be paying off this purchase for as many as thirty years, more than one-third of the average life expectancy.

For many people this asset will turn out to be one of the best investments ever, because land prices historically rise over time and because the government essentially helps you pay for your house by offering tax breaks on the interest you pay and on the profits you earn when you sell.

But not everyone is a home owner. Not everyone necessarily wants to be a home owner. And those who think they might want to be home owners are sometimes stuck in neutral trying to figure out if the cost of home ownership is worth the expense and effort.

So let's start with renting versus buying.

You Might Be a Renter if . . .	You Might Be a Home Owner if . . .
you don't expect to live in one place very long or you want the freedom to pack up and split in an instant.	you expect to set roots in your community and want the feeling of permanency in your life.
you have no interest in unclogging toilets, fixing leaky roofs, terminating the termites, or manicuring the lawn—and no interest in paying for any of that.	you like unclogging toilets and tinkering with things around the house, or you enjoy gardening and lawn work (or at the very least don't mind paying for it).
the thought of carrying tens, and more likely hundreds, of thousands of dollars of debt makes you nauseous.	the thought of dumping thousands of dollars a year into a landlord's pocket instead of increasing your own net worth makes you nauseous.
you enjoy the amenities of apartment living, such as swimming pools and playgrounds for the kids and a work-out room or handball court that you otherwise couldn't afford to purchase separately or build into your house.	you want the tax break Uncle Sam offers on the mortgage interest you pay each year, as well as the opportunity to accumulate as much as $250,000 in profits ($500,000 as a couple) tax-free when you sell.
you don't mind that your rent will increase over time.	you love the fact that your house payment will never change, assuming you have a fixed-rate mortgage. ✎ *page 71*

Over short periods of time, renting can make much more sense than buying because the cost of buying includes not just the price of the house but a litany of expenses that every middleman along the way hits you up for: points and loan-origination fees, escrow fees, legal fees, courier fees, notary fees, property taxes, title insurance, and private mortgage insurance if you don't pony up at least a 20% down payment. Then when you go to sell, you have a bunch more fees to pay. All those fees diminish, or can entirely wipe out, any profit you might have earned by selling your house for more than the original purchase price.

Over the long haul, however, it's hard to argue against joining the landed gentry. Home ownership creates wealth over time even if you buy at the top of the market. Prices might fall or stagnate at some point, but over a long stretch of time, your house is almost certain to rise in value simply because of inflation.

Inflation, or the tendency of prices to rise over time, drives the value of real assets higher—that is, real estate. All the land that has ever been made is all the land that currently exists. Inflation may crimp the value of your money over time, but it is very kind to assets such as real estate.

SO WHAT CAN I AFFORD?

That's *the* question every would-be home owner ponders.

Figuring out whether you can afford a new television or refrigerator is pretty easy. Just look in your checkbook or your bank account to see how much money you have. But most Americans generally don't have a few hundred thousand lying around that they can use to go out and grab a nice little cottage to call home.

This is going to take a loan—a mortgage, in homespeak.

Before digging into the question of what you can afford, let's step back to understand what a mortgage is, how it works, and the two basic types that exist. After all, the real question isn't how much house you can afford, it's how much mortgage you can comfortably pay each month.

Every mortgage is comprised of three traits: size, term, and rate.

Size refers to the amount of dollars you need to borrow to buy the house you want.

Term is how many years you will take to repay those dollars. The most common fixed-rate mortgages are for terms of fifteen and thirty years. Adjustable-rate mortgages, meanwhile, are fixed for anywhere from one to seven years, before their rate begins to float for the remainder of your mortgage.

Rate represents what the lender charges you for borrowing the money. Fixed-rate mortgages never change; adjustable-rate mortgages fluctuate annually, generally, though some adjust as frequently as every thirty days.

This is how size, term, and rate come together to buy you a home:

Let's say you want to buy the average American house for $250,000 in mid-2005 when interest rates on a fifteen-year and thirty-year fixed-rate loan are 4.9% and 5.4%, respectively.

With the fifteen-year note your monthly payment is $1,963.99.

With the thirty-year note your monthly payment is $1,403.83.

The thirty-year is cheaper. Great. I'll take that one.

Not so quick. You're paying that $1,403.83 over 360 months. Thus, you'll spend a total of $505,378 to buy a house with a price tag of $250,000. In contrast, you'll pay just $353,518 over the life of the fifteen-year loan, a savings of $151,860.

In short, a shorter-term loan is pricier but saves you money over the long haul; a longer-term loan means you have a smaller payment or that you can afford more house, since $1,964 over thirty years would buy you a $350,000 home instead.

Here's a handy chart you can use for reference when you're out house hunting. This shows the monthly cost for every $1,000 you finance, based on various interest rates over fifteen or thirty years. Just divide the home's price by 1,000 and then multiply that figure by the appropriate number in the chart.

EVERY $1,000 FINANCED WILL COST . . .					
%	15-year	30-year	%	15-year	30-year
4.00	$ 7.40	$ 4.77	7.00	$ 8.99	$ 6.65
4.25	7.52	4.92	7.25	9.13	6.82
4.50	7.65	5.07	7.50	9.27	6.99
4.75	7.78	5.22	7.75	9.41	7.16
5.00	7.91	5.37	8.00	9.56	7.34
5.25	8.04	5.52	8.25	9.70	7.51
5.50	8.17	5.68	8.50	9.85	7.69
5.75	8.30	5.84	8.75	9.99	7.87
6.00	8.44	6.00	9.00	10.14	8.05
6.25	8.57	6.16	9.25	10.29	8.23
6.50	8.71	6.32	9.50	10.44	8.41
6.75	8.85	6.49	9.75	10.59	8.59
			10.00	10.75	8.78

For instance, if you're financing $250,000 at 6% over thirty years, divide $250,000 by 1,000 and then multiply the result, 250, by $6.00. This way when an effusive Realtor is raving about how great your family will feel in the Average American Home, you'll know if your family's income can really swing the $1,500 monthly cost.

THE AMORTIZATION SCHEDULE

When you take on a mortgage, your lender will generally provide you with an amortization schedule that shows each of your monthly payments stretched over the life of the loan, with part of the payment earmarked for principal (your ownership in the house) and the other part going to interest (the lender's money). You'll notice in the early years that the interest payments are a much bigger portion of your note, while in the later years the principal payments are far beefier. That's the way loans are structured—lenders recoup their money first.

Back to that $250,000 house. With a monthly note of $1,498.88, here is what the amortization schedule looks like for the early months of the first year and the final months of the last year:

Month	Principal $	Interest $
1	248.88	1,250.00
2	250.12	1,248.76
3	251.37	1,247.51
358	1,476.22	22.26
359	1,484.00	14.88
360	1,491.42	7.46

ARE YOU PREAPPROVED OR PREQUALIFIED?

When you go shopping for a home, this is one of the first questions a real-estate agent will ask. It's the agent's way of determining either how serious you are about finding a home soon or how much house your lender is willing to help you buy.

Without doing any math, you already have a very good notion of how much house you can afford. However, seeking a bank's stamp of approval before you seriously search for your next home can make the home-buying process easier on you, particularly if you're hunting in the high end of your comfort range. You'll know exactly how high you can bid on a home, and you won't risk being disheartened when you find the home of your dreams only to learn a lender denies your mortgage application because it doesn't think your finances can cover the monthly note.

Both prequalification and preapproval connote something different, and it's good to know which means what.

Prequalification is an informal agreement in which a lender gives its opinion of how much money you'll be able to borrow based on the information you've provided. This is not a pledge to provide this amount of money because at this point the lender has not determined whether the information you have provided is correct. The prequalification letter costs nothing, and you have no obligation to use this lender if you stumble onto a mortgage offer with better terms. As such, a letter of prequalification is less valuable since real-estate agents and home sellers know there is still a chance your application will be denied.

Preapproved is a much more formal agreement because the lender goes through the trouble of checking your credit report and the employment and financial information you provided. Sellers in particular are often more inclined to deal with potential buyers who are preapproved since it means your mortgage application is likely to be funded quickly, accelerating the sale. As such, the preapproval letter is the better bet, though you should know that some lenders charge for this.

WHAT WILL A LENDER LEND ME?

Mortgage companies examine two particular ratios in calculating how much house you can afford:

- **Front-end ratio** is your total monthly mortgage payment divided by your monthly gross income. In general, the industry figures that no more than 29 percent of your gross income can be allocated to mortgage expenses, which include payments for principal, interest, taxes, and insurance—your so-called PITI—since those expenses constitute the ongoing cost to keep the home. If you earn $60,000 a year, or $5,000 a month, your PITI shouldn't exceed $1,450 $(5,000 \times 0.29)$.

- **Back-end ratio** is your total monthly debt divided by your gross monthly income. The industry guideline is generally in the 41% range. Total debt includes the PITI you're looking to assume as well as monthly credit-card payments, car notes, student loans, child support, alimony, tax liens, and such. With $5,000 in monthly gross income, your back-end total cannot exceed $2,050. ✎ *page 74*

Now, just because a lender or a Realtor announces that you can afford the Taj Mahal based on your income doesn't mean you should (a) buy that much house or (b) pay attention to a blathering lender or Realtor. They have a vested interest in your buying as much house as they can shoehorn you into. But only you know how truly comfortable you will be with the larger mortgage payment every month.

If when house hunting you know that you are comfortable paying $1,500 a month, but the lender tells you that your income and debt load qualify you for a house that costs $2,000 a month, you have to ask yourself: "Will I worry about paying that much money? Will that affect my ability to afford other things in life such as traveling, eating out frequently, going to movies, or investing for the future?" If the answer is yes, then ignore the sales pitch and stick to your guns. After all, it's not the lender or the Realtor who will be making your house payments.

PMI

Unless you put down a minimum of 20% of the purchase price, a lender will likely require you to pay for private mortgage insurance, or PMI. This insurance compensates the lender in case you default on your mortgage and your property doesn't fetch enough to pay off the loan balance in foreclosure.

PMI costs roughly 0.5% to 1% of the underlying value of your mortgage and is automatically built into the monthly note. On a $250,000 mortgage, PMI adds between $104 and $208 to your monthly housing cost (250,000 × either 0.005 or 0.01 ÷ 12).

If you pay PMI, pay close attention to the equity you accumulate through the years—including the rising value of your home. Once your equity tops 20% of the value of your house, your lender no longer needs the policy, though the company

FIXED RATE VERSUS VARIABLE RATE: WHICH IS BETTER?

In many ways this is a matter of personal preference based on your expectations of how long you're going to live in a particular house and what direction you think interest rates are going.

Home owners who plan to be in their house for a long time or who want the certainty of a monthly house note that will never change are best suited for a fixed-rate mortgage. You are guaranteed to pay the same note, month in and month out, with no fluctuations. The rates on fixed-rate mortgages generally are higher because the lender is committing the money to you for as much as thirty years, uncertain of where interest rates will be decades from now. Your monthly note might seem steep early on in relation to your income, but as your salary progresses through the years, your note will grow increasingly smaller in terms of its impact on your income.

Adjustable-rate mortgages, called ARMs, typically start out much lower than the prevailing market rates charged on fixed-rate mortgages. The rate on an ARM is fixed for some period of time, ranging from one month to seven years or so. After that period of time, the rates can adjust up or down, based on the movement of some index such as the prime rate or Libor (the London Interbank Offered Rate). The adjustment on most ARMs happens annually. ARMs also typically have "caps," meaning the rate cannot change by more than, say, two percentage points in any given year, and no more than ten percentage points over their life. All of that is spelled out in the loan document, though be sure to ask your lender before you get to the point of signing.

ARMs are best suited to home owners who expect to live in a particular house for a relatively short period of time. If, for instance, you expect to move in five years, it makes sense to get a five-year ARM charging 4.5% rather than a thirty-year-loan at 6.5%. Your monthly note will be smaller during the period in which you live in the house. Moreover, ARMs can be smart options when interest rates are falling since the loan is cheaper to begin with and the risk of your rate going higher is nonexistent. However, they are much riskier when rates are rising. And if you end up living in a house longer than you expected, your mortgage payment will rise at some point unless you refinance—but even then you risk facing higher prevailing rates.

A note of caution: Have your lender run a worst-case scenario showing you what your payments would look like if the rates capped out at their maximum level. Ask yourself if you could afford to live with that. If not, then an ARM may not be for you.

that services your mortgage isn't likely to ring you up to announce this. You should call and demand cancellation.

Let's say you buy a $280,000 home and put down $30,000, or 11% of the value. You'll owe PMI. But look what happens in three years if the value of your home has climbed to $301,000 (a fairly normal 2.5% annual price growth). During that period you'll have accumulated more than $10,200 in additional equity through the principal you're paying in your monthly note (this assumes an interest of 5.75% for thirty years on the $250,000 loan). That means you have equity now of your original $30,000 plus the $10,200 you've accumulated plus the difference between the $301,000 value and the $280,000 cost, or $21,000. Your total equity is $61,200, or 20.3% of your home's value (61,200 ÷ 301,000). You've passed the threshold.

By law, lenders are supposed to cancel PMI when your payments have reduced your loan balance to 78 percent of the value of the home at the time you bought it. That, however, doesn't take into account the rising value of your home. On the loan above, you need to reduce your outstanding balance to $195,000 (250,000 × 0.78) to finally axe the PMI payment. Based solely on your original purchase price and the amount of equity you gain with each monthly payment, you don't reach that level until the third month of the thirteenth year.

You'll have paid PMI ten years longer than necessary. Even if it is $100 a month, that's $12,000 wasted.

You'll probably need to have your home appraised before the lender will agree to cancel the policy, but you'll recoup that cost of a couple of hundred dollars in just a few months, and then you'll be saving money for many years.

HOW TO AVOID PMI

You can dodge PMI from the get-go with various types of loan structures if you're comfortable doing so. For instance, you could pursue a so-called 80-10-10 loan or an 80-5-15. With such a loan you take out a first mortgage of 80% of the home's value, put 10% down, and cover the remaining 10% with a second mortgage, which is sometimes structured as a standard mortgage and sometimes as a home-equity loan (more on those in a moment).

The second mortgage often carries a higher interest rate, but you still generally end up paying a smaller monthly note this way than if you were paying PMI.

The benefit of this split-loan approach is threefold: (1) You avoid PMI, (2) you build equity quicker since part of both the first and second mortgage payments are going to your principal, and (3) you get a bigger tax write-off since the interest paid on the second note is deductible while PMI is not.

CLOSING COSTS

Sometimes a kid goes into a store with $5 to buy a toy that costs $4.99, and then he is dumbfounded to find that he has to pay $5.39 because of the tax. Well, closing costs often leave home buyers equally dumbfounded.

Like that kid, home buyers sometimes are so consumed by the sticker price that they don't think about all the extras they're responsible for when buying a home. Those costs can really add up. Here are a few:

TAKE THE POINTS AND SAVE

Paying points to get a lower rate will save tens of thousands of dollars over the life of your loan. The calculations below assume a thirty-year, $250,000 mortgage in which you pay no points and get an interest rate of 5.75%, and one in which you pay two points to lock in a rate of 5.25%. Each full point typically reduces your rate by 0.25%, though that's not universally the case. You can pay a fraction of a point to more than three points depending on the cash you have available and how low you'd like your rate to be.

No Points			Two Points		
Up-front Cost	Monthly Payment	30-year Total Cost	Up-front Cost	Monthly Payment	30-year Total Cost
$0	$1,458.93	$525,215.57	$5,000	$1,380.51	$501,983.33

Paying two points hurts up front with the $5,000 outlay, but in the end you save more than $23,200.

* **Points or loan-origination fees.** This is a fee you owe the lender for providing the loan. Points are actually percentages, so two points would equal 2% of the loan value. Points can range from 0% to 3% or more. The fewer points you pay, the higher the interest rate you're charged. Conversely, the more points you pay, the lower the rate. If you know you'll own a house for a long time, it can be much smarter in the long run to pay a few points for a lower rate because you'll save thousands of dollars over the loan's duration. If cash is tight, however, the no-points option may be the best bet.

The good news is that the mortgage market is so competitive these days that lenders offer low rates on no-point loans. Many of the best rates are often found online at bankrate.com or eloan.com.

- **Property taxes.** No matter what time of year you buy a home, you're going to owe some amount of property taxes, either to the city in which your home is located or to the seller. Let's say your city levies taxes quarterly and you buy a house in August, midway through the third quarter. The house you're buying owes $500 in taxes every quarter. Since the seller owned the home for half of the quarter, the seller owes half the taxes. You owe the other $250, which will show up on the closing documents. Note that property taxes are generally wrapped into your monthly note and are paid for you by the company that services your loan, which isn't necessarily the lender since lenders frequently sell off the loans they make. However, when arranging the loan, you can request to pay your own taxes, though that might cost a small setup fee. The benefit is that you retain control of the money through the year and can invest it as you wish until taxes are due.

- **Escrow fees.** These will cost anywhere from a few hundred to a few thousand dollars. Escrow is simply an account where all the money you put down on a home is kept while you and the seller haggle over various issues before the closing takes place. Neither side has access to the money.

- **Home owner's insurance.** We'll cover this more in the Insurance section, but when it comes to closing on a mortgage, your lender typically will require that you pay for an entire year's worth of home owner coverage. You'll want to arrange this before closing because obtaining insurance coverage on a house can take a few days. Going forward, your insurance premium will be wrapped into the monthly note, and the loan-servicing company will renew your policy each year with the funds you've paid through your monthly note. Both the insurance and tax portions of your mortgage payment go into an escrow account in your name (which is not the same escrow account that was used for the real-estate transaction); it is used to pay the taxes and pre-miums. As with property taxes, you can arrange to pay your insurance yourself, again keeping control of your own money during the year.

- **Title insurance.** This is another lender-mandated cost. This policy ensures that the house you're buying can legally be bought. Title companies search various city and county records to make sure you'll own "clean title" to the house. Perhaps a divorced couple owned the house you're buying, and the husband is selling it to you. Maybe the wife has no clue. In that case she might still own legal title to the house. Rare, yes, but you don't want to fall into such a situation. Title insurance prevents it.

- **Notary fees,** courier fees, overnight fees, copy fees, sanitation fees, dog-walking fees. Okay, that last one isn't really going to show up, but you'll be surprised at how many niggling little fees pop up on the closing documents, ranging from $25 to a few hundred dollars. People want to be paid for their small part of your home ownership dream.

The message: Always show up at the closing with your checkbook in hand, just in case.

REFINANCING YOUR MORTGAGE

Between the late 1990s and 2004, Americans were on a refinancing binge. Interest rates fell to historic lows, and with each downward tick, legions of home owners rushed to their nearest lender, eager to refinance their mortgage. Some refined two, three, or more times.

It's a very wise move financially since you're locking in lower rates than you're currently paying, reducing your monthly note and, ultimately, the amount of money you must repay.

SHRINK YOUR MORTGAGE— ONE EXTRA PAYMENT AT A TIME

This is a very easy way to dramatically slice the amount of money you ultimately repay to your lender: Simply make one additional monthly payment a year.

All of that money goes to your principal; none goes to interest. That has the effect of reducing your principal, which in turn reduces the amount of interest you ultimately owe your lender. Sticking with that $250,000 average American home and the 6% fixed-rate mortgage over thirty years, one extra payment a year cuts sixty-six months off your mortgage, or 5.5 years. More important, you save $61,389 in interest.

If you don't think you can cover an extra mortgage payment all at once in a given month during the year, you can ease the pain by dividing your current monthly note by 12 and include that extra amount in each check to your lender. So if you're paying $1,500, factor into your spending plan the extra $125 each month. It all works out the same.

Caution: Banks or mortgage companies often send junk mail offering to arrange for you bimonthly mortgage payments in which your monthly note is split in half and deducted directly from your checking account every two weeks. In essence, this is exactly the same as making one extra monthly payment a year (26 half payments equals 13 full payments, 1 full payment more than 12). The catch is that the bank or the mortgage company charges you a fee for this service.

That makes no sense for someone interested in accumulating wealth. Why pay a fee for a very simple task you can accomplish on your own with no added effort?

To determine how much you might save by increasing your monthly payment, check out the mortgage calculator at www.hsh.com/calcamort.html.

When you refinance, you trade one mortgage for another, essentially taking out a new mortgage to repay the balance on your existing mortgage. Home owners refinance for several reasons: to lower their monthly payment; to pull cash out of their house (called "cash-out refinancing"); to transfer from one type of loan to another, for instance moving to a fixed-rate instead of an ARM; or to combine a mortgage and, say, a home-equity loan taken out years ago into one lower-priced note.

Before the advent of online mortgage shopping and the cut-rate fees that lenders now charge, refinancing your mortgage generally didn't make sense unless rates fell at least two percentage points below your existing mortgage rate. When mortgage fees are low, just about any respectable drop in interest rates can be a good enough reason to refinance. To determine if refinancing your mortgage makes sense, you can find all sorts of mortgage refinancing calculators on the Internet, including a pretty good one at Bankrate.com. But cost-benefit analysis is fairly easy to figure out yourself with pencil and paper or a spreadsheet. ✎ page 82

(A) Current Payment	_____
(B) New Payment	_____
(C) Difference (A – B)	_____
(D) Total Fees	_____
Months to Recoup Costs (D ÷ C)	_____

Simply subtract the size of your new payment from your current payment and then divide the total fees by the cost difference. The result shows how many months it will take to recoup the expense of refinancing. Save $100 a month on a refinancing that costs $3,000 in total, and you'll recoup that outlay in less than three years. "Total fees" includes any points or origination fees you'll pay, application fees, credit checks, attorney's fees, title search, inspections, and the like.

Some advisors will tell you a refi makes sense only if you can save at least $150 a month. Maybe. But if your mortgage is still fairly young and you expect to be in your home for many years—or for the duration—saving even $50 a month means real money over time. Can you use an extra $600 a year, money that otherwise would go to your lender?

When Not to Refinance

If you have lived in your house for years, say a dozen or more, you're at the stage where you're really beginning to eat into the principal. By the end of year twelve on a thirty-year mortgage, for instance, roughly one-third of your payments are paying down your principal. If you refinance even for just the remaining eighteen years, your benefits are fairly slim unless the interest rate difference is dramatic. You certainly don't want to refinance into another thirty-year mortgage; you're foolishly taking on a huge additional debt burden despite the lower payments.

Also, if you're refinancing to access equity in your home for consumer wants such as electronics, a car, a vacation, or a boat, you're making a mistake. In pursuing this strategy you are replacing an asset with a consumable that ultimately depreciates or has no residual value despite its psychic value. That falls into the bad-debt camp without question.

Home-Equity Loans Versus a Home-Equity Line of Credit

These are two means to the same end: tapping the equity in your house. The difference is in how they are structured.

Assume that seven years after buying your average American home its value has increased to $300,000. Over the same time your monthly mortgage payments have decreased your outstanding mortgage balance to $224,098. The difference— $75,902—marks the equity in your home, the amount of money in excess of what you owe. To access the money for any purpose, good or bad—home repairs, a swimming pool, consumer purchases, to pay off high-rate credit-card debt—you can go to a lender for a home-equity loan or a home-equity line of credit.

- **Home-equity loan.** This is a fixed-rate loan very similar to a mortgage, though their life span (the term) typically runs from five to no more than fifteen years. This is a one-time transaction, meaning you receive a lump-sum payment equal to the amount of equity you wish to draw down. As you pay off the loan, your account balance progresses toward $0.00. The interest rates on these loans tend to be higher than with a home-equity line of credit; a $50,000 home-equity loan in April 2005 carried an average rate nationally of 7.36%. But your payment will never change.

- **Home-equity line of credit.** This operates much like a credit card in that you have ongoing access to all your equity all at once or just bits and pieces over time as you need it—whenever you need to draw on the account for various financial needs. As you pay if off, your credit revolves, meaning it recycles back into your available credit line for you to draw on again if needed. A line of credit has a life span, too, and when the term expires, the outstanding balance must be paid in full. Rates on a line of credit tend to be lower, but they float, meaning they ebb and flow with the interest rates in the broader economy. That means you might borrow at 4% but end up repaying at 6% or 7% or more. In April 2005, a $50,000 credit line charged 3.59%.

With both a loan and a line of credit, the interest is generally deductible on your taxes because the debt is secured by your home.

Perversely, lenders are often eager to grant a credit line when you don't need the money but are less inclined to approve one when you do need the money because your need, by definition, often arises at moments when your finances are the tightest. A good rule of thumb: If you think you might ever want to siphon off some of the equity in your home, it makes sense to establish a credit line early.

WHEN YOU SELL: THE COMMISSION

When it comes to what you pay a Realtor to sell your house, the key word is *negotiate*. Home sellers often don't realize that the commission real-estate agents earn for marketing and selling a house is negotiable. For eons the industry charged 5% or 6% of the selling price, and home owners have come to accept that as a fixed rate for the services provided.

It is not fixed. And don't accept it.

The Internet has pushed down the cost of marketing a home because increasingly buyers are going online to find houses. That's a much more efficient way to reach eyeballs than a For Sale sign, newspaper ads, open houses, and the free real-estate pamphlets you find on street corners and in grocery stores. Meanwhile, discount real-estate firms are springing up to offer online many of the same services that traditional agents do from brick-and-mortar offices, but the discounters charge much lower commissions, some as little as 2%. On a $250,000 house the difference between 6% and 2% is $10,000, potentially a big portion of the down payment on your next home.

Full-service agents counter that they provide additional services such as arranging an open house to get potential buyers in the door, or they hold agent lunches at your house to get their peers talking up your property to clients. That's all well and good, but there's little reason to pay thousands more for services you can get much cheaper from a more efficient operator.

At the end of the day a full-service agent doesn't want to lose a potential commission, realizing that 2% of anything always beats 6% of nothing. If an agent knows you're willing to take your business to the low-cost provider, that agent will be motivated to negotiate, even down to 2% in some cases. Do not agree to pay anything above 4%—and push for 3%. You get the benefit of the added service without the marked-up cost.

IN THE DRIVER'S SEAT: CARS

You can say this for Americans: We love our cars.

As 2005 began, the folks who track car sales statistics predicted that Americans would buy nearly 17 million new cars over the course of the year. The average price was approaching $30,000.

No matter how you view it, cars are pricey. But unless you live within walking distance of everything you need or have access to round-the-clock, comprehensive mass transit—that is, basically, unless you live in Manhattan or the District of Columbia—you're probably going to need a car. And unless you have a big chunk of money you can use while still maintaining an adequate emergency savings account, you're going to have to settle for a small, inexpensive compact or a used car, or you're going to have to borrow money or consider a lease.

Logically, the smartest option financially is almost always to go for the inexpensive new car because (a) it's affordable, (b) it's under warranty, meaning you probably won't have major repair bills to worry about as you might with a used car, and (c) it will feed your psychic need for a new car—why is that new car smell so addicting?—rather than a car someone else no longer wants and that has strange stains on the driver's seat.

Yet car buying, like love, is rarely an exercise in logic. It's all about the emotion. That being the case, then, it's disingenuous to tell you that you should not look at a car as an asset but as a depreciating if not well-styled collection of metal, plastic, and glass. Equally ineffectual, no matter how accurate, is insisting that it is unwise to borrow money to pay for something that loses value the minute you drive it off the showroom floor. Such messages resonate with the clarity of a whisper at an auto race.

So let's look at car buying from a more practical perspective: with the assumption that if you're going to buy one no matter what some guidebook tells you, then you need to effectively negotiate a better price and find better loan terms. In the end, both will lower the cost of car buying and save you money every month. Recognize, of course, that a car is not an asset and that through a loan you will pay increasingly more for something that is worth increasingly less. With a lease you are effectively renting a car and signing a contract that binds you to certain, often pricey hidden obligations and that is costly to get out from under if you ultimately don't like the car.

Let's start with buying.

WHAT'S IT REALLY WORTH?

Paying the sticker price on a car is like failing to haggle with a carpet vendor in Marrakech—you've gypped yourself. Think about it. What do all those car commercials advertise? The MSRP, the manufacturer's *suggested* retail price. A suggestion is an invitation to negotiation.

So first things first: Know exactly how much car you can afford and negotiate from that point downward. If you play the games car salesmen want to play, you inevitably end up overpaying for the car and the car loan. Instead, never discuss what you can afford on a monthly basis; dealers use scads of ways to structure a car note to meet or slightly beat your monthly payment needs. Yet what you pay each month is simply the end result of two variables: price and loan terms. And dealers always manage to get you what you need without ever really addressing those issues. So slough off a salesman's glad-handing and focus your efforts on the sticker price.

To negotiate on price, you must be armed with information about the true value of the car you want with all the options you demand. The Internet has made that very easy. A variety of Web sites now offer detailed consumer information comparing the dealer's invoice cost against the MSRP printed on the window sticker. Three to check out are www.nada.com, the National Automobile Dealers Association site; www.kbb.com, the Kelley Blue Book site; and www.edmunds.com, which helpfully provides not just an analysis of the MSRP and the invoice prices but shows what consumers are paying for your exact car in your geographic region.

Pay attention to the destination and delivery charges, the necessary fees for getting a new car from the manufacturing plant to the dealer. Some dealers will inflate that number to get a little extra profit into the price. The actual charges are spelled out on the Web sites. Do not pay a penny above those charges. Also, be very wary of dealer add-ons such as dealer-applied rustproofing and other such nonsense. You're paying for something you don't need on a modern car. And if ever you see on a sticker price a charge for "ADM," immediately subtract that from the total. That stands for "additional dealer markup," pure profit the dealer is building into the price. Never, ever pay that.

At the end of the day you should never pay more than 3% to 5%, at most, above the invoice cost. What you're doing is negotiating the dealer's profit over invoice, not negotiating your cost under MSRP. If it is late in the model year, the new cars are coming out, and a dealer has lots of inventory of last year's models still hanging around, particularly those that aren't selling well, you should pay barely above invoice at all since the dealer has a clear incentive to negotiate—to make room for the new cars. If after doing your homework and if after negotiating you still think a dealer is asking too much, walk away and find another showroom. No one has ever gone broke saving money.

CAR LOANS

If you're going to finance a car, you're going to use an auto loan. They operate exactly like a home mortgage in that they're based on three variables: the principal (the size of the loan),

ONE MAY BE THE LONELIEST NUMBER, BUT ZERO IS MORE EXPENSIVE

In 2005, Ford Motor Co. offered buyers of its economy-priced Focus an incentive: $2,000 cash back or 0% financing over thirty-six months. The thought of not paying interest to buy a car, essentially using the car maker's money for free, is enticing. Instead of throwing $13,230 at a car, the sticker price on the Focus ZX3 S, you could let that cash sit in your account and earn interest while you paid off the loan. And if you didn't have the cash to begin with, well, at the very least it means your payments are smaller.

Or not.

Paying the interest in this case is a much better bargain.

Car companies always offer this *or* that. It's rarely both. Choose to use the car maker's money for free through 0% financing, and the dealer isn't likely to cut you any slack on the sales price. With the 2005 Focus, the 0% rate meant a monthly payment of $367.50 for three years. But taking the $2,000 discount and paying 2.9% for the same three years, your payment is just $326—a savings of $41 a month, or nearly $1,500 over the life of the loan. You'd have to accept interest rates of near 10.5%—well above new-car rates at the time—before your monthly payment equaled what you'd pay under the 0% scenario.

The message: Run the numbers before you run to the dealer. Price all your options to determine what saves you the most money—even if it means passing up free money. *page 96*

the rate (the interest you pay annually), and the term (how many months you have to repay the principal).

Auto lending is a very competitive market. Banks and credit unions are eager to underwrite auto loans, and all the car makers have in-house consumer finance units. To keep car buyers flocking to the showrooms, those in-house financing companies frequently provide incentives such as 0% financing, or

0.9%. Don't just jump at that low rate. Remember, this is usually an either/or proposition—either you get the low rate and pay the sticker price, or we haggle on price but you pay a higher interest rate. As such, you might be better off finding outside financing and negotiating that better price.

Before you go car shopping, though, the question you really must ask yourself isn't how much car you can afford but how much car loan you can afford. The answer is on your spending plan, which is in the upcoming Budgeting section.

You must determine how much discretionary income you generate each month and how much of it you're willing to earmark for a car. That ultimately determines how much car loan you'll be able to cover comfortably every month for the next three to four years.

Assume for a moment that you can afford $300.

The next step is to talk to your bank or credit union to find out what rates they're currently charging on new-car loans for thirty-six and forty-eight months. You don't want to stretch your notes out too far, particularly not out to seventy-two months. A six-year car note will make you feel as if you're paying on this vehicle forever, and there's a pretty good chance you're going to want to trade your car in before the loan is paid off. That means you'll either have to come up with a lump sum to pay it off when you trade in your old car (cash you could otherwise use to buy your new car), or you'll have to wrap the remaining balance into your new loan, extending the debt even further. Let's assume bank rates are 4.5% for thirty-six months and 5.25% for forty-eight months, which were available in the spring of 2005.

The next step is to check the Web sites of the various car manufacturers you're interested in. They all list the various incentive programs currently in play. This is information that will make you a far savvier consumer when it comes time to negotiate.

You now have all the necessary data to determine what you can afford in order to stay within your budgeted monthly note.

Dozens of auto loan calculators are on the Internet, but if you have a computer spreadsheet, you can do it yourself with a very simple "present value" calculation. Here's the coding:

Cell A1, type **payment;** Cell B1 type **$300,** your budgeted car note.

Cell A2, type **rate;** Cell B2 fill in the interest rate—let's use **5.25%.**

Cell A3, type **term;** Cell B3 fill in the number of months you'll pay this loan—let's use **48.**

Cell B4, type this formula: **=PV(B2/12,B3,−B1).** That's the present-value calculation used by Microsoft Excel. Other spreadsheets might be different, but they all have a basic present-value function.

The result: $12,963.04.

Now, $12,963 isn't necessarily the price of the car you can afford. That's the size loan you can afford. To that amount you must add any cash you're going to put down on the car as well as the value of any trade-in you have. If you have $5,000 in cash and a jalopy worth another $2,000, you can afford a $20,000 car, approximately. If you have no cash and no trade-in, then you can afford only $12,963.04.

By the way, you can play with those numbers in various combinations to see how increasing or decreasing the interest rate and term affects what you can afford. For instance, if you figure you can afford $325 instead of $300 by cutting from your budget one restaurant meal each month, and the dealership is offering special 0.9% financing, you can afford a loan of $15,316.90, which with your cash and trade-in means you can afford a $22,000 car.

What sort of car might that buy? Edmunds.com, among other Web sites, categorizes new cars by price. A Ford Mustang would be in your $22,000 range, as would a Jeep Wrangler, a Honda Accord, and a Mini Cooper, among many others.

The point is this: By doing your homework and working from the bottom up, starting with how much car loan you can afford, you're prepared to walk into the dealership confidently, armed with knowledge of what your car costs, its fair selling price, what financing is available, and the precise impact it will have on your spending every month. You have become a savvy car shopper. Although you're still borrowing money for a depreciating asset, you're limiting the impact on your spending to what you can comfortably afford. ✎ *page 93*

AUTO LEASES: CARJACKED IN THE SHOWROOM

This is a real ad: "Lease the all-new 2005 Jaguar X-type 3.0 liter for $399 a month for 39 months. . . ."

Ads like that are hazardous to your wealth.

If you must resort to a lease to afford the car you want, you are shopping way out of your league. Moreover, there's a very good chance the dealer is taking your wallet for a ride.

Regardless, Americans in abundance pursue car leasing because we are an aspirational lot. We see luxury all around us, and we want it; an auto lease is the ticket to a world we otherwise cannot afford. That's because the big selling point of auto leasing is that it allows you to get into a car at a substantially lower cost than you'd pay if buying it outright. Take that $399-a-month Jaguar, for instance. That lease required a $2,999 upfront payment on a car with a sticker price of $34,995. If you bought that car using the same $2,999 as a down payment, paying the going interest rate of 5.25% and paying the car off over the same thirty-nine months, your note would be $896. Can you afford that?

Consumers get mugged by leases every day because they are intoxicated by the prospect of driving such a nice car at such affordable prices, yet they don't understand the inner workings of the contract. They assume that if you're not buying the car, you don't need to dicker over price. After all, you're not paying for the car, you're just renting it. Moreover, all those TV commercials make it seem as if the monthly lease price is preestablished—see the Jaguar ad above.

Yet your monthly lease is determined by the price you negotiate on the car. Dealers never point that out, of course, because they want you to focus on the affordability of the monthly note—$399 for a classy Jaguar. $399!—not the marked-up price you're paying.

Once you understand how leases work, you realize that once again the monthly note is a red herring.

Leases are built around three factors: capitalized costs, residual value, and interest rate.

"Capitalized cost" is the agreed-upon sales price, which you have power over through your negotiating skills.

"Residual value" is what the dealer expects the car's value will be when you return it at the end of the lease term in two to five years. You don't have direct control over this, but many auto Web sites list which cars retain their value the best. This, as you will see in a moment, is important data.

Interest rate is obvious. If you're going to lease a car, check with various lenders to find who is offering the best terms. You don't have to use the dealer's in-house financing.

With a lease you pay the difference between the capitalized cost and the residual value. In effect, you're paying for only that portion of the cost you actually use—basically the cost of the car on the showroom floor minus the depreciation that happens during the years you drive it.

By negotiating a lower sales price and concentrating on vehicles that retain the most value, you can shrink the gap between the capitalized cost and the residual value. Then, by shopping for the best lease terms, you lower your interest rate. Combined, you reduce your monthly note, saving substantial dollars.

Accept the lease rate noted in the ad or the one the salesman offers, and you're basically being carjacked legally.

During the lease your auto insurance might be more expensive because your lender actually owns the car that you're leasing. Some lenders require higher liability limits or $0 deductibles, which make for pricier policies.

At the end of the lease you either return the car to the dealer or buy it for the residual value. In returning the car you could still be on the hook for thousands of dollars. Most leases limit your driving to between ten thousand and fifteen thousand miles a year. Go above that and you're hit with additional fees of between ten and twenty cents per mile. So on a five-year lease in which you rack up twenty thousand miles a year instead of the ten thousand your lease allotted, you could owe another $10,000 when you return the car. Any excessive wear and tear, and you'll be billed at a premium price as well. Tires don't match? You'll need to replace them so that they do.

Moreover, the end of the lease forces you to act. Unless you no longer need a ride, you must either buy this car or another car, possibly at a time when you don't have the money to do so. If you don't have the cash, well, you're looking at another lease.

In most cases, leasing a car just doesn't pay off in the end. Savvy consumers are better served buying an affordable car outright. ✎ *pages 97 & 101*

BANKRUPTCY

We started this chapter with the question: What is debt? Let's end it by talking about the ultimate consequences of what uncontrolled debt can lead to: bankruptcy.

Bankruptcy, in the most straightforward legal sense, is the complete or partial inability to repay creditors the money you owe. When you file for bankruptcy, the Federal Bankruptcy Court essentially stands guard over you, protecting you from creditors that might otherwise come after you or your assets, garnish your wages, or foreclose on your home.

Consumers file for bankruptcy for any number of reasons: extended unemployment leading to an inability to pay the mortgage or other bills; unexpected medical expenses with no health insurance or with a policy that doesn't cover all the costs; the acquisition of too much consumer debt through credit cards, a mortgage that's too big, or a car lease or car loan that stretched too far; marital problems.

In filing for bankruptcy, certain debts are completely discharged while others remain intact. Debt that can usually be discharged includes credit-card balances, medical bills, auto loans, unpaid utilities, and back rent. Debts that generally can't be discharged include alimony and child support, outstanding federally insured student loans, unpaid state and federal taxes for the past three years, and traffic and criminal fines, among others.

While bankruptcy can be a clean start, it comes with a high price: You lose valuable assets, and the bankruptcy follows you on your credit report for a decade, increasing the cost of living your life. For that reason, bankruptcy should be the debt-management tool of last resort.

Consumers have two bankruptcy options, Chapter 7 and Chapter 13.

Chapter 7 is a liquidation. This is the most common form of personal bankruptcy because all eligible debt is wiped away. You, the debtor, turn over all your nonexempt assets (see below) to a bankruptcy trustee assigned by the court. The trustee then sells off your assets and distributes to your creditors (those to whom you owe money) whatever proceeds are raised. The debts are then wiped out except those noted above that can't be erased. The process takes about three to six months, in most cases, making Chapter 7 quick.

Chapter 13 is a reorganization. This can drag on for three to five years, but you keep your property. You file with the court a proposed reorganization plan that describes how you intend to repay what you owe, in whole or in part. The judge decides whether to accept the plan or can insist that you modify it. If accepted, you make regular payments out of your future earnings for three to five years. You might have to repay some creditors in full; some only partially; some not at all.

What Are Nonexempt Assets?

In bankruptcy you're allowed to retain certain personal property. Most states protect a certain amount of home equity, though some states shield the entire value of your home. You're generally allowed to keep your home furnishings and clothes, as well as pensions and the money in your retirement savings plans. For that reason, if bankruptcy is unavoidable, don't raid your retirement accounts to raise cash, and don't listen to a counselor or creditor who might urge you to do so. That money is out of reach.

What's Better, Chapter 7 or Chapter 13?

That depends on your means and your assets.

Chapter 7 is quick and is best suited for debtors who don't have a lot of property to hold on to or who don't have a job or stable employment.

You must have regular income to file Chapter 13 since it is predicated on your abiding by a repayment plan. Moreover, with Chapter 13 your secured debt (backed by assets such as your car or house) cannot exceed $871,550, and your unsecured debt (credit cards, medical bills, student loans) can't top $290,525. (Those numbers were set in 2005; they're likely to change over time.) If you have filed for bankruptcy within the past six years, you have to file Chapter 13. If you have valuable nonexempt property that you want to keep—artwork, recognized collectibles and antiques, or even rental property— Chapter 13 will allow you to keep them. Chapter 7 will liquidate them.

THE NEW AND IMPROVED BANKRUPTCY: HARDER TO FILE

In early 2005, Congress approved, and President George W. Bush signed, a bankruptcy overhaul bill that had been debated for years but that was never passed. The bill the lawmakers finally approved made it more difficult for debtors to erase their debts.

Under the new arrangement, individual debtors with income that exceeds their state's median income level must, in most situations, file for Chapter 13 bankruptcy rather than Chapter 7. That means consumers will have a much more limited opportunity to wipe their slate clean of debt and will be held responsible for repaying more of what they owe.

The law also tightens the homestead exemption, preventing those who know they're going to file for bankruptcy from dumping all their assets into a pricey home in states that keep the entire value of the house out of reach of creditors.

Finally, you must also, at your own expense, meet with a credit counselor in the six months prior to filing for bankruptcy, and, before any debts are discharged, you must take a money management class.

With Chapter 13, however, your spending is severely limited to only what is necessary to live on, with the rest earmarked for debt repayment. If you miss a payment, you can be held in breach of the court, meaning the judge can insist that instead of paying back the agreed-upon 50% of your debts, you now must repay it all. Also, while many people go into Chapter 13 expecting to make good on their plan, the majority don't.

CHAPTER 3

BUDGETING

Without question, *budget* is the four-letter word of personal finance.

People despise budgets, and they despise the word because it immediately conjures feelings of confinement, as though it's because of their budget that they can't live the life they think they deserve. So even though everyone generally recognizes that they need a budget, budgets nevertheless are, like New Year's resolutions, usually abandoned fairly quickly.

Yet budgets don't have to feel constricting. Budgets can be liberating. They show you exactly what you're spending on items—and where—that might not actually matter as much to you as something far more important. You just don't realize you can afford that far more important something because of all the money you spend every day on the truly insignificant.

Let's start this chapter on budgeting, then, by rethinking the word itself. Instead of "budget," let's think in terms of a "spending plan."

Yes, you're just playing word games with your brain, since a budget and a spending plan share the same goal: to help you manage your income better. However, how your brain relates to money psychologically determines how successful you are in sticking to your budget. If your brain tells you that you feel frustrated with a plan that doesn't let you spend what you think you can afford to spend, then your budget isn't long for this world. If, on the other hand, your brain tells you that you're feeling satisfied, that you're using your money the way you think it should be used, then you're far more likely to hew to the path you've established for yourself.

SPENDING PLANS VERSUS BUDGETS

So what exactly is a spending plan, and how does it differ from a budget?

In essence, a spending plan matches your known income each month with your fixed costs and then allows you to determine how you want to spend or save the leftover money—your discretionary income—every month. By comparison, most people use their budget just to get a rough idea of how their fixed costs—those big, monthly items such as a mortgage, rent, car notes, and utilities—match up against their income. Then they try to cram the remaining dollars into categories based on historical patterns. The thinking goes something like this: "If I spent $100 a month on average last year on magazines and newspapers, I had better budget for that this year."

Never mind that you rarely read the daily paper during the week because you had no time in the morning or that your magazines piled up, untouched, because you were too tired or too busy in the evening. Maybe instead of budgeting that $100 by default you should find a more productive use for the money. That's where the spending plan comes in. page 14

A spending plan shows you exactly how much money you can spend each month on variable costs for dinners out, spur-of-the-moment purchases, a wardrobe makeover, and newspapers and magazines, or how much you can funnel into savings or toward paying off credit-card and other debt. Knowing exactly what you have to spend—and, more important, where you spend it—gives you power over your money by providing the analysis necessary to stop spending wastefully and start spending smartly. That's the spending plan's biggest advantage over budgets: You're in control of your money instead of feeling as though your money controls you.

Many guides to successful budgeting like to pump you up by describing how easy it is to cut excess expenses from your budget by simply resisting the urge to splurge on a $5 cappuccino every day. Stick to such a budget long enough, and by golly you'll accumulate enough money to buy a small coffee-producing nation one day.

And that's great—if you can stifle that yearning to caffeinate.

But that's precisely the problem. Budgets don't drink coffee; you do. Once a budget starts making you feel guilty for spending on small pleasures, you'll quickly abandon the little tyrant; this, in turn, will probably leave you feeling as though you failed again at corralling your finances. Fear of failure can be so paralyzing that you just wipe your hands of budgeting altogether, an attitude that resigns you to a life of financial vulnerability because you'll have trouble saving for what you really want, building an emergency account to tide you over a bad stretch, possibly causing you to become dependent on—or saddled by—credit to fund your life.

Spending plans are more user-friendly, though they take two or three months of acclimation. They can be complex, or they can be simple. Whatever the case, the secret to sticking to your budget is spending your discretionary dollars on what is most important to you and eliminating what you know you can live without. When that happens, your budget becomes integrated into your thinking about money, and you inherently know how unexpected purchases will jibe with your spending plan. That's where spending plans really stand apart from budgets. Since you draw up a spending plan at the beginning of every month—instead of annually, as most folks typically do with a budget—you have the flexibility to switch your plan on the fly without throwing off your spending. For instance, friends invite you to their beach house for the July 4 weekend. The excursion, you figure, will cost about $200. You take a quick peek at your spending plan and see that you had penciled in $250 for new clothes to update your wardrobe. So now you have a choice: clothes that you can put off buying until next month or later in the year, or a holiday weekend with friends?

Without the ability to see such choices in black and white on their budget, most people simply do both, either taking on debt by whipping out their credit card or dipping into their savings. They do so because the human brain has an immense ability to compartmentalize. We spend on the clothes we need and immediately put that expense behind us, forgetting about it because it's in the past. The trip is in the future, so that comes out of future money that will come in our next paycheck. We book the trip; we can afford it. The problem is that both the clothes and the trip come out of the same pot of income for the month. The result: You wreck your spending for the month.

That's the wrong path to financial success.

To give you a better sense of what you've already spent in the month and what you still expect to spend, you need a tool that gives you a visual indication of where you are at any point during the month. The chart on the next page is pulled from the companion workbook and is a small slice of a larger spending plan.

With such a plan, one glance and you know instantly where you are financially during the month. This approach helps you keep your spending on track; it helps you to remember during the month how much you have already spent on various discretionary items and what expenses are still to come. Knowing what you've already spent and what you haven't yet spent allows you to adjust your spending on the fly when those long-weekend trips and other impromptu offers pop up.

For the first few months, putting together a spending plan will seem tedious and will take some time because you must acclimate yourself to the process. By the third month, however, you'll know the process; by then, many of the variables won't

HOME	Projected Month Total	Week 1	Week 2	Week 3	Week 4	Actual Month Total	Over/ Under Projection
Rent/mortgage							
Home insurance							
Telephone							
FOOD	Projected Month Total	Week 1	Week 2	Week 3	Week 4	Actual Month Total	Over/ Under Projection
Groceries							
Dinner out							
Weekday lunch							
TRANSPORTATION	Projected Month Total	Week 1	Week 2	Week 3	Week 4	Actual Month Total	Over/ Under Projection
Car payment							
Auto insurance							
Gasoline							

change and you'll have your plan in place in the time it takes to watch a sitcom.

IN CASE OF EMERGENCY

How much does your life cost each month?

Most folks don't know that answer, though it is essential to your financial security. Right now, comb through your checkbook and look at the last six months, taking note of every expense you made that allows you to live. This inventory will largely mimic the fixed-cost list you prepare for your spending plan, but with a key difference: You won't include such things as cable or satellite TV, or high-speed Internet subscriptions since these are not necessities. They do not keep you alive or keep you sheltered; they do not educate your children or insure your life and property.

MONEY UNDER YOUR MATTRESS

Stashing cash beneath your mattress is supposedly the epitome of financial naïveté. But if you have ever been without access to cash, having money you can immediately tap at home is most reassuring.

In the vast blackout that darkened parts of the Midwest and Northeast in the summer of 2003, many automated teller machines were as useful as a train on a dirt road. The same goes for credit and debit cards. With no juice to power the machines, your cash was stuck—albeit safely—at the bank but entirely out of reach if you didn't have a checkbook; even if you had your checkbook, many merchants balked because their electronic cash registers couldn't process your check, as many registers do now.

Thus, even in a world where plastic can buy you nearly anything you need and money whips through the ether electronically, cash remains king. For that reason, keeping a few hundred dollars in a very secure spot in your home is the epitome of financial preparedness. Even if you can't get the ATM to spit money at you or get the greengrocer's debit-card reader to acknowledge your PIN, you can still buy the groceries you need to feed yourself and the family. Cash, despite being old technology, is always accepted with a smile.

The sum of this inventory is what it takes to fund your life in an emergency—if, say, you or a spouse lost a job, and you suddenly needed to pare your expenses to the absolute minimum for some period of time. You should set aside money for that possibility and hope you never have reason to draw on it.

The question is: How much is enough? That answer is different for different people in different situations. For those in careers with a large, ongoing demand or who have relatively strong job security, three months' worth of expenses is probably enough of a cushion. Those with bigger career demands, such as higher-paid managers and executives or couples who work in the same industry or at the same company, might want nine months to a year's worth of expenses in the bank. Yes, that's a lot of money to save, but financial security is a game won by those most prepared to outlast the tough times.

Remember that if you're married, the chances you and your spouse will be laid off at the same time are slim (unless you're in the same industry or at the same company). One person's continual income means the family's emergency stash either doesn't need to be as large or it can stretch further. Moreover, if you own assets such as stocks, bonds, or mutual funds held outside of a retirement savings plan such as a 401(k) or IRA, that, too, is money you can tap in an emergency.

Subtract the total monthly fixed costs from the income of the spouse with the smallest paycheck (you're planning for the worst, the loss of the highest-paying job). Whatever remains is what you need to cover each month from an emergency account or from other assets such as stocks and bonds that you can sell quickly. Multiply that amount by the number of months you think you need to create an adequate security blanket, and you have your emergency fund goal.

Where should you save your emergency funds? A money-market account. This is money you need to keep liquid. It doesn't exist to rack up big returns but to provide a sense of financial security. Still, you can let it work for you as best it can. FDIC-insured money-market accounts at online banks such as ING Direct (www.ingdirect.com) or EmigrantDirect (www.emigrantdirect.com) provide some of the biggest returns for money-market funds. As of mid-2005, EmigrantDirect's variable rate savings account yielded 3.25%, more than six times what a typical savings account yielded at an average bank branch.

THE EMERGENCY THAT CRIED "WOLF!"

Ever feel as though your auto insurance or home owner's pre-mium just jumps up unexpectedly to wreck your budget? Do you ever open your property tax bill and wonder, "Where am I going to find this kind of money?"

You're not alone, and you're not planning.

Insurance premiums and property taxes are known as fixed costs, just like the rent. They are *not* an emergency expense, as too many consumers treat them. Their nasty little attribute is that they're gen-erally billed quarterly, semiannually, or annually, and most people don't plan for them until the bills arrive, and then they have to scramble—only to scramble all over again a few months later.

To avoid all this scrambling, and to keep your spending plan on track, include semiannual and annual payments in your monthly fixed-cost cal-culations. Instead of paying your insurer or the tax assessor monthly, how-ever, put that money in your savings account or, better yet, open a separate account (either a money-market account or a basic, no-fee checking ac-count) and deposit the money there.

Then when insurance premiums or tax bills arrive, you have the money ready to go. You're not fretting about where to find the money, you're not raiding your savings account, and your budget for the month is entirely unaffected.

Moreover, by putting that sum into a money-market account, even if it is just temporarily awaiting its call to action in a few months, you earn extra money by way of the interest payments. And if there is one adage to remember when it comes to money, it's this: Money at work is better than man at work.

CHAPTER 4

INVESTING

In the spirit of everyday personal finance, this chapter isn't a treatise on the inner workings of Wall Street or the esoterica of cash-flow analysis and coupon payments. Instead, we'll approach investing from the vantage point of an average saver mainly interested in understanding the basics of stocks, bonds, and mutual funds bought and sold through either a traditional or an online brokerage firm.

The upcoming chapter on Planning will cover a variety of issues regarding 401(k) plans and Individual Retirement Accounts. This is the chapter to help you better understand all the investment options and terminology when it comes to managing those accounts or any brokerage or mutual fund accounts you might open. It will also help you decipher what all those pundits on the business news shows are talking about when they discuss why particular stocks are attractive or overpriced, what is meant by "value" or "growth" mutual funds, and why it is that bond prices fall when interest rates rise.

Don't be intimidated. Investing truly isn't all that difficult as long as you're not chasing hot tips from Uncle Mordecai, trying to time the market's up and downs, betting on penny stocks, or buying and discarding shares of companies as you would a lottery ticket, just hoping your number is plucked from the barrel. All of that is more accurately called gambling, and the books you want to read are in the gaming aisle.

If you stick to tried-and-true investment principles and devote a few hours each year to reviewing your accounts and making any necessary changes to how you allocate your assets (and we'll explain how easy that can be), your portfolio will serve you well over the long run.

WELCOME TO WALL STREET

The media throw around the term *Wall Street* in such a generic way nowadays—"Stocks surged on Wall Street today . . ."—that the place almost seems mythical, like the fabled Main Street, U.S.A.

Exist it does, however—a short little lane with the East River at one end and Trinity Church, on Broadway, at the other. And there at the corner of Wall and Broad streets stands the New York Stock Exchange, a neoclassical colonnaded building where beats the world's financial pulse. Every business day more than one billion shares of stock trade hands the old-fashioned way: open outcry. Men and women in variously colored jackets stand around a collection of booths at which particular stocks trade, verbally detailing their need to buy or sell for clients—that's you, the investor—a certain number of shares of stock at a certain price. When the price at which a buyer is willing to buy and a seller is willing to sell matches, a trade is executed, launching all manner of back-office maneuverings to ensure that the shares move from the seller's account into the buyer's account and that the appropriate amount of money moves in reverse.

Despite its concrete geography, however, Wall Street really is a state of mind, a catchall phrase for the entirety of the investment universe—stocks, bonds, mutual funds, exchange-traded funds, variable annuities, and everything in between. Wall Street pulls into its orbit not just the New York Stock Exchange but the American Stock Exchange and the Nasdaq Stock Market; it pulls in the abundance of brokerage firms, ranging from the big full-service houses like Merrill Lynch &

Co. and Morgan Stanley to the online brokerage firms like E*Trade and Fidelity Investments; it embraces the multitude of mutual fund companies like Vanguard, AIM, Janus, and Franklin-Templeton; and it includes any number of big and small banks, like national giant Bank of America and Iowa's tiny Ames Community Bank, that have their own local investment departments inside branches in towns the size of New York City and Huxley, Iowa, population 2,500.

Wherever the action takes place, the lingo is the same. So let's take a look at what it is that Wall Street is talking about.

Brokerage Firms

Essentially, two types of brokerage firms exist: full-service and discount—although the bright line that once separated those two has faded, in many instances, to little more than the remnants of sidewalk art after a rain.

Full-service: Also known as a "traditional" firm, a full-service brokerage house represents the roots of Wall Street—firms that employ brokers who ring you on the phone every now and then with an investment suggestion, or who you call when you come across some stock, bond, or mutual fund you'd like to buy or research. They employ teams of research analysts assigned to cover various companies or industries; they scrutinize financial reports and conduct field research to determine whether a particular stock is a buy, sell, or hold. Some of that research is good. Some is pretty lousy. Some is outright hype.

For the added hand-holding and the access to research, you pay more than you do with a discount firm. Exactly how you pay depends on what type of services you need or use.

- **Commission-based:** These are best for investors who only want a broker to bounce ideas off, who want a broker to call with investment ideas generated by the firm, or who want access to the research reports the firm's analysts produce.

These types of accounts are growing increasingly rare at full-service brokerage firms, however. Investors who want basic buy and sell services and an account in which to hold their shares are better served at a discount firm where trading costs are cheaper. Moreover, brokerage firms don't make much money off buy-and-hold investors who trade only a few times a year. For that reason many big-name brokerage houses are shifting clients into fee-based accounts.

- **Fee-based:** These are best suited to investors who trade a lot or who want access to lots of hand-holding, advice, and a suite of financial planning services without having to pay a fee for every transaction or each service. Instead, the brokerage firm charges a single flat fee for everything you do during the course of the year. The fees are deducted from your account quarterly, and their size depends on your so-called assets-under-management, or how much money you have on deposit with the brokerage firm. As your account grows, the size of the rate charged decreases. You might pay about 2% a year, or $2,000, if you have $100,000 on deposit, but only 1%, or $10,000, if you have $1 million. Brokerage firms push these accounts because they get paid no matter what you do, even if you do nothing, and no matter if your account is up or down for the year. For that reason, if you're not an active trader or don't require lots of services, fee-based accounts can be a waste of money because just to break even every year you have to overcome the 1% or 2% the firm is eating up—which is not always a given in volatile markets.

Traditional brokerage firms serve different, though often overlapping, markets. Some, like Goldman Sachs, cater to institutional investors such as mutual funds, corporate pension plans, and foundations, or they deal with very wealthy investors known as "high-net-worth" or "private clients"—basically folks with multiple millions of dollars to manage. Mainstream firms, while they often manage high-net-worth dollars, too, are the province of so-called average investors, or Main Street investors. These brokerage houses are the well-known firms that advertise all over television and magazines—Merrill Lynch, Morgan Stanley, Prudential Securities, Citigroup, to name a few. They tend to have a national clientele.

Regional brokers, meanwhile, also appeal to the Main Street crowd; they just don't have the same breadth in terms of their reach across the country, concentrating instead on particular geographic markets. This group includes firms like Raymond James and Morgan Keegan in the South, A. G. Edwards in the Midwest, Edward Jones in smaller markets, and Ferris, Baker Watts along the mid-Atlantic seaboard.

Discount: These firms are generally geared toward do-it-yourself investors who make their own investment decisions, who don't want unsolicited phone calls pitching 100 shares of some flea-bitten company, and who want to execute their trades themselves. Commissions are substantially less, and discounters now seem locked in an ever-escalating battle to offer the cheapest trades. Some commissions are as low as $1.95 plus ½ cent per share.

Because discount firms don't have brokers who must be paid part of the commissions they generate, because they don't employ expensive research analysts, and because they historically offer a narrower menu of services, discounters can charge those substantially smaller commissions.

But where discounters were once very utilitarian companies focused almost religiously on low-cost stock trading, they have in recent years begun to resemble in some ways full-service brokerage houses. The breadth of products they offer now extends well beyond stocks into mutual funds, bonds, options, certificates of deposit, annuities, life insurance, and so on. They offer college and retirement planning services, provide checking accounts and credit cards, and in many cases have tag-teamed with a full-service firm or two to offer clients online access to stock market research reports. Charles Schwab & Co. offers its own version of proprietary buy, sell, and hold advice—still a rarity among discounters—assigning school-like grades of A, B, C, D, and F to roughly three thousand of the largest companies. Moreover, discounters offer an abundance of stock- and mutual fund–screening capabilities as well as news alerts and even electronic bill-pay options if you want to pay bills out of the cash in your account. Fidelity Investments, dipping further into the full-service playground, will even manage your portfolio as long as you pony up at least $50,000.

Because of the cost savings, discounters are the best option for investors who are comfortable with managing their own account and doing their own research, or who don't trade frequently. Then again, if you do trade frequently, discounters may be a better option as well. Many specialty online firms have sprung up to provide very fast trader-oriented Web sites that allow you to trade directly in the market instead of routing your orders through a middleman, the route taken by most traditional stock transactions. This means that if you see an order on the screen to sell 100 shares of Apple Computer at $36.06 and you want to buy those shares at that price, you can hit that order directly without waiting for your brokerage firm to execute the trade for you.

Also, a discounter is for you if you have less than $100,000 to manage. Many full-service firms are increasingly pushing aside those relatively small accounts to focus on larger accounts that generate bigger profits for the firm. If you still want the personalized service and don't mind paying for it but your account is shy of 100 grand, consider a regional full-service firm. They're more likely to want your business.

WHAT'S YOUR STYLE?

On Wall Street—there's that generic use—investment pros frequently talk about "style," though as you might surmise this has nothing to do with Donna Karan or Ralph Lauren. They're

MAY DAY ON WALL STREET

The world as Wall Street had known it for decades changed forever with the opening bell on May 1, 1975, a Thursday—what has come to be known in the brokerage industry as May Day. On that morning, at the mandate of the Securities and Exchange Commission, brokerage firms deregulated their commission structure. Before May Day, commissions were set in stone. With deregulation, brokerage firms were free to charge what the market would bear.

While many full-service firms used May Day to *increase* their commissions, a then-small California outfit by the name of Charles Schwab & Co. bucked the trend, undercutting rivals by as much as 75%. Schwab, in doing so, radically altered the notion of a brokerage firm. Unlike full-service peers, Schwab didn't provide research or employ brokers to solicit trades from customers. Instead, Schwab simply served as a no-frills gateway to stock trading for do-it-yourself investors who didn't want the sales spiels or the often boosterish research.

That fashioned an industry now populated by numerous discount brokers as cutthroat as the airlines. When one firm lowers its commissions, the others often rush to follow. As such, where trading 5,000 shares of a particular stock once cost an average of $3,500 (about 70 cents a share), today that same trade at some deep-discount online brokerage firms costs about the same as a McDonald's Happy Meal.

✥

talking about the various styles of stock picking that different investors rely on. Think of it this way: Are you a dog person or a cat person? Vegetarian or carnivore?

Whichever you answer, the choice begins to define your perspective. The same holds true with investing. Some investors lean toward stocks with earnings that are growing rapidly; they're "growth" investors. Others go for stocks that appear to be undervalued compared to their financial prospects or the assets they own; these are the "value" investors. Some want a

BROKER VERSUS ADVISOR

Starting in the 1980s and accelerating through the 1990s, brokers recast themselves into the role historically played by investment advisors. To many individual investors the distinction is semantics. Broker, advisor—as long as I'm getting good investment advice, who cares?

But there is a difference that is important to understand: Brokers and advisors are governed by two different rules, and those rules have a bearing on your rights as an investment consumer and the obligations brokers and advisors have to you and your money.

Brokers operate under a "know your customer" standard governed by the National Association of Securities Dealers. Under that standard, brokers are obligated to offer clients "suitable" investments. What defines suitable gets very squishy very fast. While a broker would have trouble justifying the sale of a volatile Internet fund to an eighty-year-old seeking income, a broker could argue that sticking that same retiree into a variable annuity contract is suitable even though such annuities are generally ill-advised for older retirees. Courts have ruled in the past that brokers generally have no legal responsibility to look out for a client's best interest even if a client relies on the broker's advice to buy or sell a particular investment. NASD rules mandate that brokers act fairly with investors, and flouting the NASD can get a broker fined or banned from the industry. Still, shenanigans happen all the time.

Advisors operate under the principles of "fiduciary duty," a legal obligation to put the client's needs first. That's not to imply that a fiduciary duty is necessarily better or that a dishonest advisor won't rip you off. However, in disputes fiduciary obligations can be easier to argue than suitability.

Advisors also must disclose all conflicts of interest they have as well as how they are compensated, among other necessities—all of which is reported on Form ADV, which the advisor is obligated to give you. Form ADV is also available online at the SEC Web site, www.sec.gov (on the home page look for the link titled "Check Out Brokers & Advisors"). Advisors must give you Part 2 of the form, but Part 1 can be enlightening, too. It details disciplinary actions, if any, against the advisor. Part 1 is on the SEC Web site.

Brokers, meanwhile, are not obligated to hand you any particular form disclosing their potential conflicts of interest, though you can check for any disciplinary actions at the NASD Web site, www.nasd.org. Look on the home page for the link to "NASD BrokerCheck."

Many brokers are dually registered as broker and advisor and often suggest investments wearing their advisory hat and then transact for you on those suggestions as a broker. Determining what rules apply—suitability or fiduciary duty—can be challenging in such a case. Here's what to remember: The type of account you have determines the rules under which you and your broker are ultimately playing. A brokerage account is subject to suitability rules; an advisory account is subject to fiduciary duties. Here's how to tell the two apart:

You Have a Brokerage Account if . . .	You Have an Advisory Account if . . .
your broker doesn't have permission to trade without your consent, meaning it's a non-discretionary account.	your broker does have permission to trade without your consent, meaning it's a discretionary account.
any advice offered by your broker is solely incidental to the business of trading stocks and other securities in your account.	you pay your broker for advice separate from the fees or commissions charged on the account.
all customer documents, including advertising and marketing materials, clearly state this is a brokerage account.	your broker presents herself as a planner and offers financial planning services or delivers a financial plan.

mixture of both, so-called growth at a reasonable price, or GARP investors. Still others latch onto stocks that display lots of momentum and are moving higher as analysts ratchet up expectations that the company's profits will grow faster than expected—the "momentum" investors. And then there are those who, like medieval seers studying runes, try to divine the future by staring at the patterns they see in the charts chronicling a stock's historical prices over some period of the past. They are the technicians.

Growth Investing emphasizes revenue and earnings that are growing quickly and consistently and are well above average. (Revenue, or sales, is the top-line number, all the money a company generates selling whatever it sells; earnings, or profits, is the proverbial bottom-line number, all the money left over from revenues after paying salaries, production costs, taxes, and such.)

What defines "well above average" depends on the company and the industry. For an upstart technology company with a new whizbang gadget, above average might mean earnings growth of 50% to 60% a year. For a sedate grocery-store chain, above average might be earnings growth of 15% a year.

Growth investors commonly "pay up" for the stocks of companies they deem to be growth plays. That means that as long as a company is growing at a rapid clip, investors willingly pay what others might consider a high price to own the shares. For them, stock price is secondary to earnings growth because a fast-growing company will grow into—and then exceed—its stock price. It's a bit like a toddler's shoes; you buy them a size too big so that the feet have room to grow, expecting that three months later the shoes will already be too small.

As such, growth stocks often sport high price-to-earnings, or P/E, ratios. If the broader stock market, defined as, say, the Standard & Poor's 500-stock index, trades at a P/E multiple of 18 (meaning the value of the index is 18 times the combined per-share earnings of the 500 companies in the S&P index), then a growth stock might trade at a P/E of 25 or 30, or up into the 50s and well above. Take, for instance, technology favorite Cisco Systems, which at one point in late 2000 traded at a P/E multiple of up near 160 as growth investors pushed the shares continually higher, betting that technology and the Internet would revolutionize the fabric of everyday life.

While that certainly has happened, you can't escape the

risks inherent in growth-stock investing. Growth stocks are often "priced for perfection," meaning that as long as they continue to deliver the fast-growing sales and earnings, investors will continue to want the stock, supporting the share's high price. But as soon as the helium starts to leak from the balloon, watch out. Even if a company's growth slows to 45% from 50%—still considered a very rapid clip—investors will punish the stock price as they rush to evacuate what they suddenly see as a sinking ship. To wit: After eleven years of pleasing Wall Street, Cisco in early 2001 missed its earnings estimates for the first time ever—by exactly one penny per share. Revenue growth, meanwhile, had slowed to 40% from expectations of 55%. Investors clobbered the stock, which was already on its way down from the $80s after the Internet bubble burst. Cisco shares ultimately slid all the way into the single digits at one point.

Value Investing is the equivalent of those celebrated blue-light specials at Kmart where merchandise is suddenly on sale. Value investors look to buy $1 worth of assets or earnings as cheaply as possible.

Value investors buy stocks at prices that they believe underestimate a company's true profit potential or undervalue its known assets—in other words, bargain-basement investing. These stocks typically trade at a relatively low P/E multiple, often in the single digits or in the range of ten to fifteen times earnings. They trade that low because the majority of investors feel a company's earnings potential is limited or it's in a troubled industry, or maybe they're concerned about some operational or financial problems the company has or is expected to have. Value investors scrutinize stocks in terms of their relative valuation or how they currently trade in relation to their history, their industry peers, and the market as a whole. The yardsticks used are numerous, but the most common are the price-to-earnings ratio as well as measures that look at the price in relation to a company's cash flow, book value, and sales. (Cash flow is the so-called real earnings of a company since it adds back into the earnings stream noncash expenses such as depreciation and amortization. Book value is a company's net worth, which, like your personal net worth, is total assets minus total liabilities.)

Film giant Kodak is one example of value investing at work. Once a high-flying growth stock, the company's shares fell from grace in 2001 as Kodak faced increasing pressure from rival Fuji Film and as concerns mounted that digital imaging would one day supplant traditional film as the photographic medium of choice. Kodak's shares, above $90 in the late 1990s, tumbled into the low $20s by 2003. At that point value investors began snapping up the stock, confident that Kodak's business, while certainly changing, wasn't dead. The shares began to rebound—into the mid $30s in early 2005—as the prognosis for Kodak's survival improved.

Of course, the risk with value investing is that what looks like value might just be a well-dressed corpse. Bethlehem Steel Corp. was once a fallen angel that many value investors bought at hugely depressed levels of just a few dollars a share. Yet the company fell into bankruptcy, and now the shares trade only among collectors of old stock certificates.

Historically, value investing beats growth investing over the long haul, though in shorter periods growth often wins. The reason is that value investing done right has a built-in margin of safety in that the intrinsic value of the stock an investor buys is generally more than—or at least much closer to—the purchase price. Over time, value, like cream, rises to the surface. Growth investing typically doesn't provide that safety margin. While growth dishes up big gains over shorter spans, companies simply cannot sustain above-average growth rates for very long. When that growth slows, their stock prices fall or stagnate, possibly for years, hurting the returns.

Technical Analysis is performed by technicians who are some of the most disparaged and least understood investment pros on Wall Street.

Growth and value investors, despite their differences, are at heart fundamental investors. In other words, they examine a company's financial fundamentals to determine whether they think a stock is a buy or a sell. Technicians, by contrast, scrutinize charts and graphs, searching out telltale patterns that, they argue, portend a stock's future performance. They don't rely on P/E ratios or sales growth of free cash-flow calculations. Instead, they seek "rounded tops" and "double bottoms" and "head and shoulder" formations in the trends that play out in a stock's daily, weekly, monthly, and yearly pricing charts. Many technicians don't even know the companies behind the stock symbols they trade. As long as a particular pattern is evident, that's all they need to know. That's why fundamental investors look upon technicians as black-box wizards or Wall Street's version of carnival freaks off in the corner reading tea leaves and playing with Ouija boards.

By examining price movements and trading volume, technicians try to determine whether an increasing supply of a particular stock or an increasing demand for those shares is winning at that moment, and then they place their bets based on that analysis. For that reason technical analysis is generally best suited for short-term trading, not long-term investing. However, long-term growth and value investors can benefit from technical analysis in that the technical buy and sell signals can give some guidance on when to get into or out of a stock.

THE INDEXES

These days nearly every corner of the stock market has an index to measure something. The Russell 2000 tracks small-company stocks. The Wilshire 5000 measures the performance of virtually the entire U.S. market. The SOX shadows the semiconductor sector, while the VIX measures market volatility. Morgan Stanley, meanwhile, indexes much of the developed world with its Europe, Australasia, and Far East Index, or EAFE.

DOLLAR-COST AVERAGING

This strategy marks a simple way to accumulate wealth over time. Every month you invest a fixed amount in a particular stock or mutual fund. Such a plan forces you to invest regularly, does not attempt to time the market, reduces market risk, and over time reduces your overall per-share cost in the stock or mutual fund.

Here's how it works: Say you really like a company and conclude that it has years of growth coming, but you can't afford to invest several thousand dollars at that exact moment. Instead, you buy, say, 100 shares initially and thereafter regularly invest $1,000 every quarter. This is what your purchase record might look like after two years:

Period	Price/Share	Shares Bought	Amount Invested
1st quarter Year 1	$25	100	$ 2,500
2nd quarter Year 1	22	45.45	1,000
3rd quarter Year 1	17	58.82	1,000
4th quarter Year 1	17	58.82	1,000
1st quarter Year 2	15	66.67	1,000
2nd quarter Year 2	18	55.56	1,000
3rd quarter Year 2	24	41.67	1,000
4th quarter Year 2	25	40.00	1,000
	Total	466.99	$9,500
	Average price per share		$20.34

Had you invested a lump sum to begin with, your stake in the company would have returned nothing over the two years. Through dollar-cost averaging, you have a profit—in this case, nearly $2,200—even though the stock has effectively gone nowhere. The reason is that you bought high, you bought low, you bought in the middle regardless of the market price of the shares. As such, you accumulated more shares when the price was low and fewer shares when the price was higher, leading to an average price per share below the cost of your original investment. The real strength of the strategy is that you consistently invest through thick and thin, which ultimately helps you build wealth over time.

Dollar-cost averaging works best with companies that allow you to make additional purchases of stock by sending in a check on a monthly or quarterly basis. This is known as a Direct Stock Purchase plan, or DSP. This keeps you from having to pay additional brokerage commissions with every purchase. A Dividend Reinvestment Plan, or DRiP, works similarly in that your dividends are automatically reinvested in the company's shares each quarter.

Www.themoneypaper.com is a useful resource for investors who want to dollar-cost average. The online firm lists all the companies that offer a DSP and DRiP option, and helps you enroll electronically in the plans in which you want to participate, though you will pay a one-time fee with each plan you enroll in.

To dollar-cost average in a mutual fund, you can either send a check to the fund on a regular basis, maybe monthly or quarterly, or arrange for the fund to routinely draw the money from your bank account on a preset schedule. Nearly every fund offers this option.

⚜

For the most part, mainstream investors and the media pay attention to the three big indices: the Standard & Poor's 500, the Dow Jones Industrial Average, and the Nasdaq Composite Index.

The S&P 500 measures the performance of what Standard & Poor's defines as the five hundred largest publicly traded companies in the United States and is considered the benchmark for the U.S. market. These stocks are widely held by investors and are spread across the industrial, transportation, utility, and financial sectors.

The Dow Jones Industrial Average, typically just called the Dow, is comprised of thirty very large stocks selected by the editors of the *Wall Street Journal,* who, on rare occasion, alter the composition to reflect the changing composition of American industry. At 110 years old as of 2006, the Dow has long been a cultural icon, arguably the symbol of the American brand of capitalism. Critics complain that the Dow's lack of breadth makes it less relevant than the S&P 500. Yet the index has proved remarkably reflective of America's economic growth and largely moves in sync with other major market indices.

The Nasdaq Composite, begun in 1971, tracks the performance of a large proportion of stocks that trade on the Nasdaq Stock Market. The index gained fame during the bull market bacchanal of the late 1990s when, on the strength of surging prices for technology, telecommunications, and Internet stocks, the index tripled in value in three years. That strength also proved to be Nasdaq's biggest weakness. The index is so laden with technology shares that it is a poor reflection of the broader market and is viewed more as a measure of the digital economy. Little wonder, then, that the Nasdaq Composite was kneecapped—ultimately falling 78%—when the stock market's technology-inspired bubble burst in 2000.

STOCKS

A stock certificate implies partial ownership of a business. That is as complicated as it gets.

Stockholders, also known as equity holders, own *common stock* and share proportionally in the profit stream of the business. If profits rise over time, then the share price tends to rise, too. If profits fall or slip into losses, the share price falls on the assumption that the business is not as valuable as before. Stockholders are also entitled to a share of any dividends a company might pay. So if you own, say, a single share in the Starbucks chain of coffeehouses, then every time someone orders a double-skim, half-caff iced mocha latte Frappuccino, an infinitesimally small sliver of the profit from that sale has your name on it. Multiply that by millions and millions of cups of coffee, and at some point you're talking real money.

Here is why that's important to you, the shareholder, and how it flows through to *your* bottom line. Remember that stocks are priced based on their stream of earnings. As that stream of earnings grows, the stock price grows even quicker because of the relationship between price and earnings—the price-to-earnings multiple, or P/E. If a stock has a P/E of 15, then every 10-cent increase in the earnings generally moves the stock's price by $1.50 (15 × 0.10). If a high-growth stock with a P/E of 50 earns an extra $1 per share, then the share price roughly jumps by $50.

Now, a P/E ratio isn't constant; it ebbs and flows based on overall market conditions and how valuable investors think a particular company's earnings stream is on any given day. But the point remains that earnings ultimately drive a stock's price because earnings represent the reason a company exists—to generate profit. That profit, in turn, marks the reason investors own the stock and the mechanism by which they value the shares.

As a stockholder you have voting rights in the company, with one share typically representing one vote. If you own 100 shares of Starbucks, then you have one hundred votes in every matter the company puts before its shareholders—be it the election of the board of directors or a proposal to merge with another company.

Stockholders have the greatest potential for reward but also accept the most risk for loss. If a company excels in its business, then the value of just a relatively few shares of a company can turn a small sum of cash into substantial wealth. On March 13, 1986, had you been prescient enough to see what the future would bring, you could have purchased 100 shares of Microsoft stock at between $25.50 and $29.25, the price range in which the software giant's shares traded on the day of its initial public offering, the first time the company ever sold stock to the public.

Twenty years later that original investment of less than $3,000 would be worth roughly $800,000. That's the reward side. You bought into Microsoft's stream of earnings, which, because it became the world's dominant software provider, grew exceedingly fast. That, in turn, propelled the value of your small ownership stake in the company.

Then there's the risk. On February 11, 2000, you could have spent $1,100 on 100 shares of Internet retailer Pets.com. Within months, as Pets.com flamed out amid the Internet bust, your shares would have been worthless—though you would have helped fund those now-famous TV commercials featuring a sock-puppet dog.

Reading the Stock Tables

Look in the stock market section of any daily newspaper and you'll find page after page of symbols and numbers in tiny agate type. The symbols define a particular company; the numbers define the price. Let's pull apart a random stock quote printed in the April 29, 2005, issue of the *Journal* to explain what can seem like a bunch of mumbo jumbo. Let's pull apart Royal Caribbean, the cruise ship company.

YTD % CHG	52-WEEK HI	LO	STOCK (SYM)	DIV	YLD %	PE	VOL 100s	CLOSE	NET CHG
10.2	29.10	16.49♦	RogerComm B **RG**	.10g	.3	dd	664	28.81	0.22
-19.6	71.36	33.87♦	RogersCp **ROG**		...	18	1529	34.65	-0.18
-3.5	50	35.90	RohmHaas **ROH**	1.00	2.3	18	9588	42.66	-0.42
9.6	19.98	14.07	RollinsInc **ROL** s	.20	1.0	22	1790	19.23	-0.47
1.6	68.09	48.03♦	RoperInd **ROP**	.43	.7	25	3627	61.73	-1.65
15.2	15	9.96	RosTele **ROS**	.50e	4.0	...	639	12.60	-0.21
3.1	33.04	20.27	RowanCos **RDC**	.25e	.9	54	29482	26.48	-0.71
-4.7	8.53	6.28	RylSunAli ADS **RSA**	.44e	6.1	...	500	7.26	-0.15
10.8	61.95	41.63	RoylBkCan **RY**	2.20g	...	...	376	59.21	0.15
-24.4	**55.47**	**37.80**	**RylCaribn RCL**	**.52**	**1.3**	**17**	**9447**	**41.15**	**-0.15**
1.7	65.11	47.68♦	RylDutchP **RD**	3.44e	5.9	12	20280	58.33	-0.15
-8.1	11.85	7.03	RylGpTch **RYG**		...	dd	61	9.62	...
-13.4	9.80	6.95	RylKPN ADS **KPN**	.45e	5.4	...	188	8.28	-0.10

To start with, stocks trade based on their ticker symbol—(SYM) in the stock table on the previous page. It is a shorthand code that investors use as a stand-in for a particular company's full name. In our case, Royal Caribbean is known to investors as RCL.

New York and American Stock Exchange–listed companies generally sport a one- to three-letter symbol; some of them seem nonsensical (such as KRB for insurer MBNA Corp.), while others seem all too obvious (BUD for Anheuser-Busch Cos., the makers of Budweiser beer) and others are just cute (LUV for Southwest Airlines, homage to the company's home airport, Love Field in Dallas, Texas). Some companies, like Dow Jones & Co., have two-letter symbols (DJ), while a few firms own a much-coveted single letter, like Citigroup's C. Rumor has it the NYSE for years has reserved the single letter M for a certain Redmond, Washington,-based software giant that the exchange hopes to one day steal away from the Nasdaq, where stocks typically carry four-letter symbols (MSFT, for instance, is the Nasdaq moniker by which investors trade Microsoft).

Start at the far left of the stock table and move to the right. The "ytd % chg" reports that RCL's stock is down 24.4%, year-to-date. The "52-week Hi-Lo" shows that RCL shares have traded as high as $55.47 and as low as $37.80 in the past year. The "div" is the annualized per-share payment that each RCL shareholder receives, in this case 52 cents per share. That number determines the "yld %," or the dividend yield, 1.3%. To get there mathematically, you'll need to skip two columns to the "close," the final price of an RCL share—$41.15—when the market closed the day before, April 28. (More on yield in a moment, but the calculation is 0.52 ÷ 41.15.) As for the columns skipped, "PE" is the price-to-earnings ratio, which will be discussed below; for RCL the current PE is 17. "Vol 100s" represents the number of shares traded; the 100s means you need to add two zeros to the end to come up with 944,700 shares that traded. Finally, "net chg" shows the dollar amount by which each share of RCL rose or fell the day before—and on this day it fell 15 cents.

THE BID-ASK SPREAD

While Royal Caribbean shares closed at $41.15, the price of the stock during the day is never just a single number. Stock quotes come in pairs, such as RCL $41.13–$41.16. That's the so-called bid-ask spread. The number on the left is the "bid," the highest offer that buyers are willing to make at the moment to own shares of RCL. The number on the right is the "ask," the lowest price that owners of RCL will accept to sell their shares.

From that spread all the action on Wall Street stems. Buyers who want the stock jump to $41.16 to own it. At that point the spread might move to $41.16–$41.18, and other buyers who want shares dive in at the higher price, pushing the spread up again. Conversely, sellers who really want to get out will jump down to $41.13 to meet those buyers, and the spread might fall to $41.11–$41.13. Then more sellers will rush to meet that lower price just to get out before the shares slip again.

In essence, the gap between the bid and the ask marks the spot where the law of supply and demand plays tug of war. When there are more buyers than sellers, demand pushes the price higher. When there are more sellers than buyers, supply drives the price lower.

PREFERRED STOCK

This is a class of company stock designed specifically to pay a set dividend every quarter. The dividend rate is based on the share's par value, the face value of the stock, or the price at which the shares were originally sold to the public.

Preferred stock gets its name because it is "preferred" to common stock in the event of a bankruptcy or a restructuring, and it has preference over common stock when it comes to

THE ORIGIN OF "BLUE CHIP"

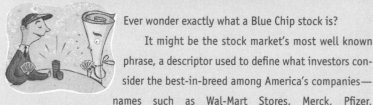

Ever wonder exactly what a Blue Chip stock is?

It might be the stock market's most well known phrase, a descriptor used to define what investors consider the best-in-breed among America's companies—names such as Wal-Mart Stores, Merck, Pfizer, International Business Machines, Anheuser-Busch, American Express, Bank of America, Microsoft, Intel, McDonald's, and Kellogg's, to name a small handful.

But why are they called chips? And of all the colors, why blue?

Well, the best explanation seems to be that the term originated in 1904 and refers to the chips used in a poker game. Anyone who owns a set of poker chips will recall that they come in red, white, and blue and that the blue ones represent the highest denomination—or, seen another way, the most valuable chips. And that's what Blue Chips supposedly represent in the stock market—the most valuable stocks, with "value" in this case implying those shares that most investors want to own for the underlying company's strength of earnings or financial stability.

Of course, you could also argue that the stock market, like poker, is often a game of chance, making the term Blue Chip even more apropos.

paying dividends. Moreover, dividends are often cumulative, meaning that if a company stumbles financially and can't pay its dividends for a while, then it still owes you for every dividend it skips. Thus, as a preferred stockholder, you will be repaid before the company can pay common stockholders. Preferred stock, however, doesn't usually have voting rights. Moreover, preferred stock has no claim on the earnings, just the dividend. That means rising or falling earnings don't directly tug on the share price as they do with common stock.

Just as common stock is known by its symbol, preferred shares are known by their dividend rate—banking giant Citigroup's 6.365% Series F shares, for instance. The stock pays a set dividend of $3.1825 per share per year. The stock's par value is $50. That makes the original dividend yield 6.365%. Preferreds typically trade as some letter in a series when companies issue more than one batch. Citigroup also had trading in 2005 series G, H, M, and V.

Not all preferred shares are equal, however, and investors must be aware of what they're getting—or not getting, as the case may be.

- **True preferred** kicks off dividends generated by the company's profit stream. As a result, the dividends qualify for favorable tax treatment, meaning they're taxed at 15%. True preferred shares carry par values of $50 or $100 and typically trade around those prices.

- **Hybrid preferred** shares, officially known as Trust Preferred Securities, pay distributions that aren't truly dividends. The payout doesn't come from profits but largely from interest payments, much like a bond. For that reason these dividends aren't eligible for the lower 15% rate but are instead taxed as ordinary income, which is usually a higher rate. Hybrid preferreds are recognizable because their par value tends to be $25.

Web site Quantumonline.com provides a list of hundreds of true and hybrid preferred stocks. You'll have to register to gain access to the data, but registration is free.

AMERICAN DEPOSITARY SHARES/GLOBAL DEPOSITARY SHARES

ADRs and GDRs, in investor slang, are the U.S.-traded shares of foreign companies—firms such as Japan's Sony and Toyota, Mexico's Cemex and Telefonos de Mexico, England's Diageo and British Airways, and Germany's Bayer.

These are companies with products or services that are often well known by U.S. investors—such as Diageo's lineup of adult beverages like Smirnoff vodka and Guinness beer—and they want access to the world's largest stock market, the United States. But for regulatory reasons Diageo can't just list in the United States the shares it has listed on the London Stock Exchange, Diageo's home market. Instead, it must create a new class of stock that is registered in and trades in the United States—the ADRs and GDRs.

For all intents and purposes an ADR is the equivalent of the ordinary shares traded in a particular company's home market. The key differences are that the shares trade in dollars instead of yen or rand or pounds, and often the shares are not one-for-one equivalents. Each Diageo ADR that trades on the New York Stock Exchange represents four ordinary shares in London; each ADR of Telefonos de Mexico equals 20 TelMex shares in Mexico City.

For investors who want international exposure through individual stocks, ADRs are the most convenient option because they trade in dollars during U.S. market hours and on U.S. stock markets and exchanges. They also tend to be some of the biggest, most significant companies from a particular country—many are global giants—meaning they have some history of successful growth through the years.

The downside is that because companies issuing ADRs are frequently big global businesses, they're often not a pure play on a local economy. Smaller, locally oriented companies are a better option for that, but they generally don't list their shares in the United States. For that you have to either invest locally (which is increasingly viable but beyond the scope of a general guide to personal finance) or go with country-specific mutual funds and exchange-traded funds, which we'll get to in a bit.

THE KEY NUMBERS

Investors are a lot like baseball statisticians: They track numbers, lots of numbers. In the case of stocks, the numbers that investors like to look at range from the obvious, such as earnings and sales, to the seemingly esoteric, such as days-sales in inventory.

A few numbers that the Street looks to with regularity are most useful to know. Here are brief definitions for three widely discussed numbers that will help you understand what your broker or advisor or best friend is talking about.

Earnings per share: The net income of a company divided by the total number of shares the company has outstanding. This is the proverbial bottom line, reported (where else?) at the bottom of the income statement in the quarterly and annual reports. Investors scrutinize this number every possible way every three months and then again annually to see if a company's profits are rising, falling, or stagnant. Rising is good. For instance, for 2004, thrift-savings giant Washington Mutual reported net income of $2.878 billion, and 884.05 million shares outstanding. Third-grade math (2,878,000,000 ÷ 884,050,000) gives you $3.26 a share—exactly what Washington Mutual reported.

Price-earnings ratio: Known as the P/E, this is the current price of a stock divided by its most recent four quarters' worth of earnings. So, sticking with Washington Mutual, in the spring of 2005 the company's shares fetched about $42 apiece. Since it earned $3.26 in the previous four quarters, its P/E ratio is 12.9 (42 ÷ 3.26). P/E ratios differ for various sorts of companies. Fast-growing technology stocks can trade at a P/E of 50 or more. A slow-growing utility might fetch a P/E in the single digits. The trick is to examine the P/E in relation to the company's historic range and against the broader market as a whole.

Dividend yield: A company's annual dividend payment divided by the stock's current price. For all of 2004, Washington Mutual paid its shareholders $1.74 for each share they owned. Thus, at $42 the stock yielded 4.1% (1.74 ÷ 42). Yields, like a P/E, run the gamut. Slow-growth industries typically have fewer investment options for the cash they generate, so they pay bigger dividends, providing a bigger yield. Fast-growing companies, meanwhile, often pay no dividends—and thus,

Condensed Consolidated Statements of Income

In millions, except per share amounts

Year ended December 31,	2004	2003	2002
Interest Income			
Loans held for sale	$ 1,472	$ 2,501	$ 1,921
Loans held in portfolio	8,825	7,668	8,671
Available-for-sale securities	764	1,738	2,951
Trading securities	151	84	39
Other interest and dividend income	138	172	273
Total interest income	11,350	12,163	13,855
Interest Expense			
Deposits	2,043	2,165	2,661
Borrowings	2,191	2,369	3,065
Total interest expense	4,234	4,534	5,726
Net interest income	7,116	7,629	8,129
Provision for loan and lease losses	209	42	404
Net interest income after provision for loan and lease losses	6,907	7,587	7,725
Noninterest Income			
Home loan mortgage banking income (expense):			
Loan servicing fees	1,950	2,273	2,237
Amortization of mortgage servicing rights	(2,521)	(3,269)	(2,616)
Net mortgage servicing rights valuation adjustments	(235)	712	(3,219)
Revaluation gain from derivatives	1,011	338	2,517
Net settlement income from certain interest-rate swaps	538	543	382
Gain from mortgage loans	649	1,250	1,375
Other home loan mortgage banking income (expense), net	(5)	127	31
Total home loan mortgage banking income	1,387	1,974	707
Depositor and other retail banking fees	1,999	1,818	1,634
Securities fees and commissions	426	395	362
Insurance income	226	188	155
Portfolio loan related income	401	439	349
Trading securities income	89	116	156
Gain from other available-for-sale securities	50	676	768
Gain (loss) on extinguishment of borrowings	(237)	(129)	282
Other income	271	373	56
Total noninterest income	4,612	5,850	4,469
Noninterest Expense			
Compensation and benefits	3,428	3,304	2,813
Occupancy and equipment	1,659	1,592	1,136
Telecommunications and outsourced information services	479	554	507
Depositor and other retail banking losses	195	154	179
Advertising and promotion	276	278	234
Professional fees	158	267	201
Other expense	1,340	1,259	1,118
Total noninterest expense	7,535	7,408	6,188
Income from continuing operations before income taxes	3,984	6,029	6,006
Income taxes	1,505	2,236	2,217
Income from continuing operations, net of taxes	2,479	3,793	3,789
Discontinued Operations			
Income (loss) from discontinued operations before income taxes	(32)	137	113
Gain on disposition of discontinued operations	676	–	–
Income taxes	245	50	41
Income from discontinued operations, net of taxes	399	87	72
Net Income	$ 2,878	$ 3,880	$ 3,861
Net Income Attributable to Common Stock	$ 2,878	3,880	$ 3,856
Basic earnings per common share:			
Income from continuing operations	$ 2.88	$ 4.20	$ 4.01
Income from discontinued operations, net	0.46	0.09	0.08
Net Income	3.34	4.29	4.09
Diluted earnings per common share:			
Income from continuing operations	$ 2.81	$ 4.12	$ 3.94
Income from discontinued operations, net	0.45	0.09	0.08
Net Income	3.26	4.21	4.02
Dividends declared per common share	1.74	1.40	1.06
Basic weighted average number of common shares outstanding (in thousands)	862,215	903,666	943,905
Diluted weighted average number of common shares outstanding (in thousands)	884,050		

have no yield—because they retain their profits to grow the business. Companies often boost—or sometimes decrease—their dividend from quarter to quarter, so you'll need to multiply the current quarter's dividend by four to annualize the payment.

BONDS

An old Wall Street saw holds that gentlemen prefer bonds.

Decades ago when that phrase was popular, it meant something since investing in stocks was derided as a fool's gamble. Bonds were for investors, in the highfalutin sense of the word, because bonds, unlike stocks, provide a certain safety of principal and typically pay a set amount of interest on a routine schedule, usually every six months.

Today, however, it's not so much the case that gentlemen—or ladies, for that matter—necessarily prefer bonds. While many bonds certainly retain the safe characteristics that attract many income-oriented investors, Wall Street has engineered all manner of bonds over the years that can be as risky as a roulette wheel and as volatile as lightning. Moreover, stocks have proven over time to provide greater returns that allow investors to stay ahead of inflation.

Bonds do have a place in any balanced portfolio, however, since they temper the risk inherent in stocks. At their core, bonds are nothing more than an IOU, a promise by a company, the federal government, or your hometown to repay you a certain amount of money over time for the dollars that you lend it. With some bonds a company or a government agency will put up collateral, an asset that secures the debt so that if the company or the government agency can't repay the loan, then you and all the other lenders have a right to claim some portion of the collateral to recoup your investment. In other cases the only asset backing the bonds is the full faith and credit of the issuer. If that issuer is a company, then repayment depends on the company's ability to generate enough income to service its debt obligation to you. If the issuer is a government agency, then repayment depends on the taxing authority of the agency or some other revenue stream that is specifically spelled out in the documents authorizing the bond issue.

Investors generally consider bonds "safe," meaning the original investment, the principal, will be returned in full when the bond matures—assuming the company doesn't default on its obligations, but more on that momentarily. Moreover, in many cases the interest payment is supported by some stream of revenue, such as a city's ability to impose sales taxes, from which the necessary income is drawn.

Maturity can be as short as a few months or, in rare cases, as long as a millennium. Safra Republic Holdings, a Luxembourg-based company, famously issued one-thousand-year bonds in 1997, and dozens of companies, led by Walt Disney Co., have sold one-hundred-year bonds. By and large, though, most long-term bonds stretch out no further than thirty years.

Because bonds are an income investment—you buy them to pocket the interest payments for several years before getting back your principal—there are two key numbers: price and yield. They are related in a slightly odd fashion: As one falls, the other rises—what's known as an *inverse relationship*. Once you see it in action, it's fairly easy to grasp.

Bonds trade at prices based on their *par value,* the face value of a bond. Most bonds are originally priced at a par value of $1,000, the price at which the bond was originally sold and the amount of money the issuer of that bond will return to the bondholder when the bond matures. Though the par value doesn't change, a bond's price can fluctuate wildly between the issue date and the maturity date. You might hear, for example, that a bond is priced at 98% of par, meaning it will cost you $980 to buy a $1,000 bond. Or maybe you'll hear that it's priced at 102, meaning you'll pay $1,020 for that bond. Troubled bonds might trade as low as 20, or $200 per bond.

Yield measures the amount of income you'll receive in the course of one year. Yield is calculated as a percentage of the bond's price. So, for instance, if a newly issued $1,000 bond yields 5%, you will receive $50 annually for that bond (1,000 × 0.05).

Now let's go back to that inverse relationship between price and yield. If you buy that newly issued bond for $1,000 and it pays you $50 a year in interest, your yield, as noted above, is 5% (50 ÷ 1,000). But if you were to buy that same bond after it had already been trading in the market for several years and you paid, say, $1,100 for it, the yield would be 4.55% (50 ÷ 1,100). You're still getting the same $50 a year; that never changes with a bond paying a fixed interest rate. It's just that you had to pay more to get that $50 annual income stream. Likewise, if you'd bought the bond when it was trading at $950, your yield would jump to 5.26%. Essentially it comes down to this: The interest payment doesn't move, it's fixed; but the bond's price moves continually. And as the price of a bond rises, the yield falls. Conversely, as the price of a bond falls, the yield rises.

IT'S ALL ABOUT THE YIELD

Individual bond investors own bonds for one basic reason: to pocket the income provided by the yield. But there's more than one yield to know.

If you buy a ten-year bond at $1,000 par value on the date it is issued and the stated interest rate is 6%, then you will receive 6% annually, or $60 for each $1,000 invested. That's the basic yield.

But what if you buy that same bond priced at 107, or $1,070, after it has been trading for three years? The bond will still pay its stated 6% rate, but you will not earn 6% annually because of the time remaining—seven years—and the price you paid for the bond.

The first yield to calculate is the *current yield,* the actual yield you earn based on the amount of money you've invested. In this case the current yield is 5.61% (60 ÷ 1,070).

But that's not what you're going to earn over the remaining seven-year life of the bond. You'll need to calculate *yield-to-maturity*, which measures your overall rate of return from the time of purchase until your principal is returned. Remember, in this example you're investing $1,070, but you'll recoup only $1,000 at maturity, so you'll have a $70 loss of principal. That loss gnaws at the interest income you will receive over the next seven years. On this particular bond, then, the yield-to-maturity is 4.81%. The calculation is rather involved. If you want to figure it out easily, search for a yield-to-maturity calculator on the Internet; you can find an easy, though detailed yield calculator at www.investinginbonds.com, which is run by the Bond Market Association. That site is also valuable because it provides up-to-date bond prices, allowing you to research a fair price for a particular bond before you buy or sell. Bond pricing can be tough to come by since thousands upon thousands of bonds exist, and not all trade with regular frequency.

Now, to complicate matters, some bonds are "callable," meaning the company or government agency that issued them has the right to repurchase them from you—call them in— before the stated maturity date arrives. Such bonds have a stated call date, so you'll know when you buy it that it can be repurchased at some point and, if so, exactly when. Just because a bond has a call feature doesn't mean it will be called. Bonds are typically called during periods of low or falling interest rates when companies, agencies, states, and municipalities have an opportunity to shrink their interest payments by replacing higher-interest-rate bonds with lower-rate bonds. To compensate investors, callable bonds are generally repurchased at a slight premium to the par value, maybe $1,100 on a $1,000 bond. Thus, if our ten-year bond can be called in year seven and ultimately is, we want to know exactly what we can expect over the next four years (remember, we bought this bond three years after it was issued). Our yield-to-call is 6.24%.

One final complicating factor: If a bond has multiple call dates, you'll need to know the *yield-to-worst*, the worst possible rate of return you would earn if the issuer calls in your bond on any of the possible call dates. Let's say our bond can also be called in the eighth year but at par value, meaning no premium, which is common when the last call is close to the maturity date. Our yield-to-worst is 4.42%.

So there it is: A simple ten-year bond with five possible yields—6%, 5.61%, 4.81%, 6.24%, and 4.42%—based on when you buy it, when it matures, and when it might be called and at what premium, if any.

BOND RISK AND RATING

Despite what safety they offer, bonds also offer risk. That risk comes in two major varieties: credit risk and interest-rate risk. To help investors gauge the risk they face in owning a particular bond, various credit-rating agencies analyze bonds and assign grades like AAA or Baa2. The higher the rating, the more unlikely it is that a bond investor will lose money when serving as a lender to a particular borrower. The lower the rating, the more substantial that risk. The two most widely followed credit-rating agencies are Standard & Poor's and Moody's Investors Service.

Credit risk is the chance that a company, because of addled finances for whatever reason, can't make the scheduled principal and interest payment it owes you. This is called a default. Companies can and do default on their bonds in troubled times, though it is fairly rare and dependent on what type of bond you're dealing with.

U.S. Treasury bonds never default because they're backed by the full faith and credit of the United States government. On the other hand, high-yield bonds, so-called junk bonds, default with some frequency. A study by Standard & Poor's, the New York company that researches and grades bonds based on the risk that investors face when owning a particular bond, reports that junk bonds initially rated triple-C (CCC) historically default within 2.8 years of being issued, on average, and nearly

29% of those bonds default in the first year. Because junk bonds have a higher level of default, investors demand greater reward for taking on the risk; they demand higher interest payments. By the way, junk bonds are those that carry a credit rating of BB or lower on the Standard & Poor's scale.

The highest-rated corporate bonds default, too, but historically that happens less than 1% of the time. State and local governments default as well on occasion—though, as Standard & Poor's notes, such defaults "are virtually nonexistent."

Interest-rate risk is more likely the risk you'll face with bonds, and it stems from interest rates moving higher. When the Federal Reserve raises interest rates to slow the economy, existing bonds lose value. That's because an existing bond that pays, say, 4% isn't worth as much to investors as a new bond paying 5%. The reason: The newer bond provides a bigger stream of income payments.

This plays out in such a way that, based on the inverse relationship, the price of the existing bond falls just enough to push the yield up to roughly match the current bond. So if a new $1,000 bond pays 5%, or $50 a year, then an existing $1,000 bond paying 4%, or $40 a year, will fall in value to roughly $800 to generate the same yield—5%—as a new bond would (40 ÷ 0.05). Because of this, owning long-term bonds at a time when interest rates are low and primed to rise can be a very risky strategy even if they are U.S. Treasury bonds, the safest in the world.

TREASURY, MUNICIPALS, AND CORPORATES, OH MY!

Bonds come in numerous varieties, but the three most common are Treasury bonds, municipal bonds, and corporate bonds. Let's dissect them individually since each one has unique characteristics.

Treasurys are United States sovereign debt, issued by the federal government to help fund the budgetary needs of running the country. Investors don't pay state or local income taxes on the interest from Treasurys, though they do pay federal taxes.

Treasurys come as bills, notes, and bonds. Bills are short-term, maturing in one year or less. The shorter the maturity, the lower the yield. In early 2005, three-month T-bills, as they're called, yielded about 2.8%, whereas one-year T-bills yielded about 3.3%. T-bills are issued at a discount to their face value. If you buy $10,000 worth of newly issued T-bills that will yield 2.5%, you'll actually pay just $9,750 and receive $10,000 at maturity. The $250 difference is your interest payment and your profit, on which you'll pay federal taxes.

Treasury notes are issued for periods of two, three, five, and ten years. Unlike T-bills, T-notes are issued at their face value and are ultimately redeemed at face value. Along the way you are paid a fixed-rate of interest every six months.

Treasury bonds, or T-bonds, are issued for periods extending beyond ten years. The most famous is the Treasury's thirty-year bond, once considered the bellwether bond, responsible for mortgage rates and other long-term lending needs. The Treasury stopped issuing these bonds in October 2001, however, and the ten-year T-note became the market's bellwether. The Treasury Department is once again talking of reintroducing the thirty-year bond.

Although most Treasurys are purchased by institutional investors and foreign governments, individual investors can buy them as well through brokerage firms and banks, and directly from the government at TreasuryDirect.gov. Brokers and banks generally charge a fee for the transaction; TreasuryDirect does not.

Increasingly popular with individual investors are Treasury Inflation-Protected Securities, or TIPS. These bonds protect your investment against inflation, which over time devalues your money. Like a traditional Treasury, TIPS pay a fixed interest rate. Unlike a traditional Treasury, however, the original principal invested in a TIPS bond fluctuates with the Consumer Price Index, the government's most widely watched measure of inflation. As inflation ticks higher, your bond's principal ticks higher as well. Moreover, as the principal increases in value, the semiannual interest payment increases, since each interest payment is based on the principal amount.

If, by chance, deflation occurs instead of inflation, then the face value of the bond decreases in value, and the interest payments are calculated using that lower principal. But there is a safeguard: If the value of the TIPS at maturity is lower than the original face value, the Treasury gives you back your original investment.

Municipals are issued by state and local governments and agencies for everything from the construction of a new water and sewer plant to new schools and hospitals or toll roads for a new airport.

Muni bonds, as they're called, typically pay interest semiannually. That interest is exempt from local, state, and federal taxes. Generally, though, you must own bonds issued by the state in which you live to be exempt from state and local taxes. If, for instance, you live in Louisiana but own munis issued by, say, Mississippi or Arkansas, you'll pay Louisiana state taxes on the income. There are exceptions to this rule: The District of Columbia, Alaska, Indiana, Nevada, South Dakota, Texas, Utah, Washington, and Wyoming don't tax income from other states' bonds.

Unlike Treasurys, munis aren't risk-free since there is the chance of a default. Moreover, credit-ratings agencies downgrade municipal debt all the time, meaning that what was an A-rated issue might slip to BBB if the municipality's finances grow tight for whatever reason. In that case, the value of the bond is likely to slip a bit since investors will push down the bond's price to increase its yield, added compensation for taking on the increased risk of default.

Still, default risk is very low. Between January 1, 1986, and January 1, 2005, no muni bond issue with a credit rating of AAA or AA—the two highest ratings on the Standard & Poor's scale—defaulted. Lower-rated municipal debt defaults more frequently, though overall the rate of muni bond defaults during the nineteen-year time span was just 0.26%.

Of all the types of bonds, munis tend to be an especially good choice for investors in a high tax bracket. Since muni bond income isn't taxed at any level, such investors won't be pushed into possibly an even higher tax bracket by the added income, and the income itself won't be reduced by Uncle Sam's bite.

Corporates are issued by companies and are sold to help finance everything from the construction of a new computer chip fabrication plant to refinancing existing debt or helping to afford the acquisition of a competitor.

Corporate bonds, like most munis and Treasurys of one year or longer, usually pay their interest payments semiannually. The biggest distinguishing factor is that income from corporate bonds is taxable on the local, state, and federal levels.

Also, default risk is greater with companies. State and local muni bond issuers generally have taxing authority, giving politicians some means of raising the funds necessary to repay outstanding debt. The U.S. government can essentially print money or borrow more to pay off what it has already issued, while cities can raise taxes broadly or narrowly by increasing sales taxes or maybe the taxes imposed on a pack of cigarettes or a gallon of gasoline. Companies don't have such options. Still, the rate of default among the highest-grade corporate bonds, called "investment-grade debt," is minuscule. At the peak in 2002—a bad period for companies and the economy—corporate default rates globally hit just 3.5%.

SMALL BONDS FOR SMALL INVESTORS

Buying bonds can be a pricey proposition for individuals since bonds trade based on par values of $1,000 or $5,000 per bond. Thus, a so-called round lot of bonds—five bonds—can run as high as $25,000. In addition, numerous individual federal, municipal, and corporate bonds exist, and many trade infrequently, meaning that pricing is often stale. That generally makes their purchase more expensive.

One way around this with corporate bonds: Direct Access Notes (www.directnotes.com) and InterNotes (www.internotes. com). These competing firms make it simple for individual investors to buy and hold corporate bonds. You buy the bonds at par value, so you're paying the same price as the big institutional investors like pension funds and mutual funds. You can buy as few as one bond, and the commission is built into the bond, so you pay no additional fees. Best of all for income-oriented investors, many of these bonds pay interest monthly instead of semiannually. That can help smooth the income stream of investors living off the income that their portfolio generates.

There are risks with these bonds: Along with the standard risks of corporate bonds described earlier, these bonds are relatively illiquid, meaning you might not get a good price if you need to sell them quickly. But if you have no need to sell them, then they can be a wiser choice than venturing into the traditional bond market.

TAX-EQUIVALENT YIELD

Because of greater default risk and the taxes owed on the interest payments received, investors generally demand a higher interest rate when buying corporate bonds. The higher rate offsets some of the risk and the tax burden, providing an incentive to bypass safer munis and Treasurys. After all, if a one-year muni bond pays, say, 3.5%, why buy a similar corporate bond that pays the same rate when you're going to lose as much as a third of the income to taxes?

But just because one bond offers a bigger interest payment doesn't necessarily mean it offers the most money at the end of the day. Remember, you may have to pay taxes. That

INDIVIDUAL BONDS VERSUS BOND FUNDS: IT'S *NOT* SIX OF ONE, A HALF-DOZEN OF THE OTHER

Odd as it might seem, owning a bond and owning a bond fund are not one and the same. The fund is riskier.

If you own a bond and hold it to maturity, you are guaranteed to get back your principal, assuming the bond doesn't default. No matter whether rates go up or down and no matter whether through the years your bond's price rises and falls from one day to the next, you will always get back your par value and earn the stated rate of interest.

That's not so with a bond fund. Since the fund is comprised of numerous bonds, and since the portfolio manager is continually buying and selling bonds in the fund, the fund has no set maturity date. Nor does it have a set interest rate.

All of this means that if interest rates are falling, an individual bond will likely provide greater income since its interest rate won't change, while the bond fund's rate is likely to begin to slide as the manager sells off certain bonds or is forced to replace maturing bonds with new bonds that will offer lower rates in a lower-rate environment.

On the flip side, bond funds can be hurt when interest rates are rising because—here's the inverse relationship at work, again—the value of existing bonds falls. That means the portfolio of bonds in the fund all decrease in price, which, in turn, drives down the fund's net asset value, its market price. As such, there's no guarantee you will recoup your original investment in a bond fund.

Over time, much of this balances out for bond fund investors. Moreover, mutual funds are a more efficient way to own bonds for many investors since you own a more diversified portfolio at a cost far cheaper than you generally would pay to buy numerous individual bonds.

However, if you want assurances you'll retrieve your principal at some future date, then you may want to own individual highly rated bonds. If you happen to own individual Treasurys purchased through www.treasurydirect.gov, which is operated by the U.S. Treasury Department, you pay no commission to buy. You will pay a $45 fee if you want to sell a bond before it matures, though if you hold it to maturity, you'll pay nothing. With a minimum investment of just $1,000 per bond you can begin to build a fairly diversified portfolio of government bonds. You'll need to open an account with TreasuryDirect.gov, and all your bonds will be held in electronic form, meaning you won't have to keep track of or store individual bonds.

If you want to own other types of individual bonds, such as municipal or corporate bonds, you will need to transact through a brokerage account.

points to a key variable when considering bonds, what you'll hear referred to as the "tax-equivalent yield." Because bonds are taxed to varying degrees, the interest rate you earn tells only part of the story. You have to subtract taxes from your interest payments to determine how much money you'll really end up with. Consider this simple example: All things being equal and all risk aside, what's the better investment—a corporate bond yielding 4.5%, a Treasury offering 4%, or a municipal bond paying 3.5%? Take a look at the following chart:

After-tax value of an annual interest payment on a $1,000 corporate, Treasury, and municipal bond. This assumes a federal tax rate of 25% and a state tax rate of 5%

	Corporate	Treasury	Municipal
Interest rate	4.5%	4%	3.5%
Pre-tax income	$45	$40	$35
Federal taxes due	$11.50	$10	—
State taxes due	$2.25	—	—
After-tax income	$31.50	$30	$35
Tax-equivalent yield	3.15%	3%	3.5%

Owning the municipal bond in this situation offers the greatest amount of income.

If you remember only a few things about bonds, remember this: As the price of a bond goes up, its effective yield goes down, and vice versa. High-quality bonds are safe in that the principal you invest will almost always be repaid if you hold the bond to maturity. But that doesn't mean bonds are risk-free since rising interest rates can shrink the value of your bond and result in losses if you sell before maturity. Finally, high-yield bonds are called "junk bonds" for a reason. You take on a great deal of credit risk that, over time, historically results in defaults. If you're going to own junk bonds in a portfolio, do so through a mutual fund that specializes in them, and even then keep your exposure to a small percentage of your portfolio.

Just to bring this section full circle and to show exactly how bonds can mitigate the risk of owning stocks, consider the fate of investors who held a portion of their portfolio in bonds during the bear market in stocks that began in 2000 and dragged on through 2001. Most stockcentric mutual funds sank during that period, some falling by big double-digit percentages. But bond funds and balanced funds performed admirably. The Dodge & Cox Balanced mutual fund, for instance, a well-respected fund that splits its investments between stocks and bonds, gained 15% in 2000 and another 10% in 2001.

So while bonds can be sedate and safe or dicey and dangerous, properly paired with stocks they provide the counterbalance necessary to build a portfolio that can weather the storms that occasionally dump on the stock market.

MUTUAL FUNDS

March 1924. In Boston, the Massachusetts Investment Trust launches America's first mutual fund.

The concept was novel but straightforward: Investors pool their money and mutually own a portfolio of investments that are, in turn, managed by professionals with the authority to buy and sell stocks as they see fit. The fund's owners share in the investment income and gain broader diversification than they could achieve on their own; in return they pay the managers a fee for their expertise.

In the intervening decades not much has changed. Mutual funds still operate in a similar fashion; the only difference is that one of every two households in America now owns shares in a mutual fund, and investors have not one but more than 8,100 different mutual funds in the United States to choose from. Combined, those funds manage about $7.5 trillion. To add some perspective, that's triple the $2.6 trillion earmarked for the U.S. budget for 2006.

Open-end Versus Closed-end

Most mutual funds are known as open-end funds. They issue as many shares as investors wish to buy. The share price is based on the value of all the assets the fund owns divided by the number of shares the fund has issued. If a fund has $10 million in assets and it has issued one million shares, then each share is priced at $10—what's known as the net asset value, or NAV, of the fund. This is the price quoted in the tiny print in the back of the newspaper business section.

If you come along and buy $1,000 of the fund, then it issues you 100 shares. The result: The fund has assets of $10,001,000 and 1,000,100 shares outstanding, which still equals $10 per share. Open-end mutual funds do not trade on any stock exchange. Instead, they're sold and redeemed by the mutual fund company itself. Unlike stocks, where prices change through the day, open-end funds price their shares just once a day, after the market closes when the fund calculates the cumulative value of all its investments. That's the price at which you will buy or sell shares.

Closed-end funds, meanwhile, trade just like shares of stock on an exchange. These funds issue a limited number of shares that trade directly between investors through brokerage firms. They, too, have an NAV, but the shares don't necessarily trade at that value. Because there exists a set number of shares, the market price is determined though supply-and-demand fundamentals. So if investors hanker to own some particular closed-end fund for whatever reason, they might bid up the price so that the shares cost more than the NAV. Similarly, if they're disenchanted with a fund for some reason, demand might shrivel, and the price would slip below the NAV.

When a closed-end fund's price is above its NAV, the fund is said to trade at a premium. At prices below the NAV, the fund trades at a discount. If you pay attention to the historical trading patterns of closed-end funds, you'll see they routinely swing between trading above NAV and below NAV. Investors often buy when the fund sells at a discount and then look to sell when the fund fetches a premium.

No-load Versus Load

Open-end mutual funds either charge a "load" or they don't, in which case they're called "no-load" funds. Loads are the sales charges a fund company imposes to pay the broker who sold the fund. Loads can be front-end, in which you pay the fee before your money goes to work for you; they can be back-end, where you pay the fee when you withdraw your money; or they can be level-load, in which the fund company takes a percentage of your return each year for five years or so.

Investors have been conditioned to rebel against loads, and for good reason. The load eats into your returns. Invest $10,000 in a fund charging a 5.75% load—a common amount—and roughly $9,425 goes to work for you. Over the course of twenty years that's a profit difference of roughly $5,550 on an investment that compounds at 12% annually, which a number of mutual funds have done. Moreover, no-load funds historically have outperformed load funds, another solid reason to overlook them.

Every rule has its exception, however, and there are instances when paying the load is the better choice. That's particularly the case when the fund manager has demonstrated a long history of besting the overall market and the fund's peers. In that case you're paying for an obvious benefit: better returns than you'd get in even a no-load fund. Paying the load can also make sense if you're truly a long-term investor and the fund's underlying fees (see Expense Ratio below) are relatively inexpensive. Your total costs over many years might actually be less than with a no-load fund that has higher management fees.

Additionally, load-bearing funds can make sense when you're investing in foreign markets, where a fund manager's ability to wade through all the various obstacles that exist overseas can be well worth the cost—as long as the fund has proved itself through long-term performance.

EXPENSE RATIO

Where loads are one-time fees that compensate the broker or financial advisor who sold the fund, expense ratios are ongoing annual fees that the fund company charges to keep the lights on, to pay the portfolio managers, to mail your statements, and so forth. Included in this are the 12b-1 fees, named for a Securities and Exchange Commission rule that allows fund companies to use a portion of the assets to pay the cost of marketing the fund.

These fees are deducted routinely from the fund's assets, thereby cutting the returns you receive as an investor. As such, you want to pay attention to the fees a fund charges. Morningstar tracks this information for individual funds at its Web site, www.morningstar.com.

Expense ratios are all over the map depending on the fund's purpose. With bond funds you typically don't want to pay more than about 0.75%, or $7.50 a year for every $1,000 you have invested. That's because the range of returns separating the good funds from the mediocre is fairly narrow, and you want to keep your expenses as low as possible to keep your returns as meaty as possible.

The same holds true for large-company stock funds, many of which have expense ratios of less than 1%. The Fidelity Spartan 500 Index fund, which shadows the S&P 500, charges a downright miserly 0.10% as of mid-2005. Of course, that's a passively managed index fund, meaning all that Fidelity must do is own the stocks represented in the S&P 500 Index; there's not much analysis or trading to contend with. Actively managed funds, those in which the managers choose what to buy and sell and when, are costlier, but many good ones charge between 0.50% and 0.75%.

Once you get into small-company stock funds, specialty sector funds, and many international funds, your cost of ownership should be no more than about 1.5% annually.

Types of Mutual Funds

Basically, you'll find a mutual fund for just about any investment strategy you can imagine. Let's look at the key types of mutual funds, starting with the most basic. (Bond funds were covered previously in the bond section.)

Index Funds are effectively armchair investments: Once you pick the indexes you want to be in, you can pretty much kick back in your armchair and watch TV. These are low-maintenance, low-cost mutual funds built to mimic the price movement of some particular stock or bond index. In fact, the largest mutual fund in the world—the Vanguard 500 Index—tracks the S&P 500 Index of big-company stocks.

With an index fund you're not relying on a mutual fund manager's ability to pick winning stocks. Rather, index funds are "passively managed," meaning the fund owns whatever the components are that comprise a particular index. There's no second-guessing. If the index changes—say it adds a stock while kicking out another—the index fund changes to reflect the new composition.

Index funds offer broad diversification within a particular segment of the market efficiently and cheaply. Instead of buying numerous small-company stocks to gain exposure to the small-cap market, for instance, you can benefit from the growth of small companies as a market sector by owning the Vanguard Small Cap Index fund that tracks the Russell 2000, the leading small-cap index, comprised of two thousand small-company stocks.

Index funds have a big advantage over actively managed mutual funds in that they don't have to pay analysts and portfolio managers to dig up investment ideas. For that reason index funds are generally much cheaper to own over time than typical mutual funds (see Expense Ratio above).

The downside is that because there's no one at the helm deciding what stocks might be better or worse than others, the best an index fund will do is keep time with the market. Good actively managed funds aim to do better than that, hoping to ultimately give you superior profits. A few succeed; many more fail.

With the proliferation of index funds—hundreds exist—you can build a well-diversified, inexpensive, and balanced portfolio without ever owning a single stock or bond. Index funds track everything from the biggest stocks to the smallest stocks. They track real estate, the corporate and Treasury bond market, international stocks, and gold, among others.

If nothing else, here's a very good reason to employ an index fund: 80% of actively managed mutual funds underperform the market as a whole. With an index fund you don't have that worry since the fund *is* the market. Of course, neither do you have the opportunity to be part of that 20% of funds that beat the market.

Balanced Funds, sometimes called "hybrid funds," invest in a mix of stocks and bonds. Through this mix the fund seeks a balance of both income (from the bonds, preferred stock, and stocks with sizable dividend income) and capital appreciation (from stocks). Balanced funds are designed to be a one-stop shop for investors who don't want to serve as their own alchemist mixing a little equity here and a little debt there to create the perfect portfolio.

In good times balanced funds don't usually run alongside the bulls, but in bad times neither do they get mauled by the bears.

Two considerations with balanced funds: First, a fund's mix can shift at any point, depending on what the manager foresees for the economy and the market, and that mix may or may not match what you want. Second, if you already own a basket of stock and bond funds individually, you've created your own balanced fund, so there's no reason to invest in one of these as well.

Life Cycle Funds target a particular retirement year in the future and invest with an eye on that date. Some target a particular mix of assets for investors who don't pick a retirement date but instead pick an aggressive, moderate, or conservative investment blend.

With the target-maturity date funds, portfolio managers ratchet back the stock exposure and increase the bond exposure as the years progress. In essence this is a more customized balanced fund, ideal for investors who otherwise don't want to muck about with their portfolios or have to figure out an appropriate asset allocation.

Life cycle funds are popular among the 401(k) crowd because of the targeted maturities. A forty-year-old who expects to retire in 2032 at age sixty-seven could invest an entire 401(k) account in a 2030 fund, one aimed at workers retiring around that year. In 2005 a version of just such a fund held 70% of its assets in domestic stocks, 14% in international stocks, and 16% in bonds. By comparison, a 2015 fund distributed assets this way: 48% domestic stocks, 7% international stocks, 39% bonds, and 6% cash.

The point of a life cycle fund is to make the fund your single investment since it does all the work determining the appropriate allocation. Thus, if you invest in a life cycle fund, don't diversify by loading up your portfolio with a bunch of other funds, too.

Sector Funds focus on particular segments of the stock and bond markets, such as an Internet fund or an emerging-market bond fund. Sector funds are typically actively managed by portfolio managers striving to beat the market by cherry-picking what they determine through their research are the best investments to own in a particular sector.

Sector funds are for investors who want broad exposure to a particular slice of the market that owning individual stocks doesn't allow for efficiently. Such funds are available for just about any piece of the market. Fidelity Investments is one of the biggest providers of such funds, covering more than forty sectors—everything from food and agriculture to air transportation and paper and forest products.

Sector funds are risky since they're myopic in their approach to investing. If pharmaceutical stocks as a group fall out of favor among investors, then the pharmaceutical sector funds get hurt. Then again, sector funds can be winning long-term investments. Of all the mutual funds that existed in the fifteen years that ended in early 2005, two of the best performing were the Fidelity Select Home Finance fund, which owns mortgage-related stocks, and the Vanguard Health Care fund. Both were up roughly 19% per year over that time period.

Money-Market Funds, commonly called "money funds," are open-end mutual funds that seek to preserve a constant NAV, or share price, of $1. The income the fund generates is paid to you in the form of additional, fractional shares. Money funds can be either taxable or tax-free, depending on their underlying investments. They are a low-risk investment—a place where savers stash cash for their emergency spending needs or to save for a home purchase.

Though they sound identical to money-market accounts from the Banking chapter, money-market mutual funds are a different animal.

Remember that a money-market account is an FDIC-protected bank account that provides relatively limited access to your money since you're allowed only a few withdrawals per month without facing fees. In contrast, with a money-market mutual fund you have daily access to your cash, but the money is not FDIC protected. Though exceedingly rare, you can lose money in a money-market fund if a fund "breaks the buck," or falls below the $1 NAV.

Pay attention to the fees, particularly in an environment where interest rates are unusually low. Like all mutual funds, money funds charge management fees that average about 0.80%, though some funds are substantially lower. With money funds in particular, even a small fee can stand out like a crow in a bucket of milk. During 2004 when short-term interest rates hit just 1%, numerous money funds rushed to reduce or waive management fees temporarily because those fees would have wiped out the paltry returns the funds provided. Web sites such as www.bankrate.com and www.imoneynet.com track money-market mutual fund returns and provide a ranking of the highest-yielding funds as well as contact phone numbers.

Exchange Traded Funds, or ETFs, are the new kids on Wall Street. They are essentially mutual funds that, like shares of stock, trade on an exchange and are priced continuously throughout the day. Most ETFs trade on the American Stock Exchange, and much information about ETFs is on the American Stock Exchange Web site, www.amex.com. The most popular ETFs have cutesy names like Cubes, Spiders, and Diamonds—the sobriquets awarded, respectively, to the Nasdaq 100 tracking stock (symbol QQQQ), the S&P 500 depositary receipts (symbol SPY), and the Dow Jones Industrial Average unit trusts (symbol DIA).

Numerous ETFs exist, and new ones pop up constantly. They track everything from the obvious indexes to the obscure: individual countries, individual industrial sectors, specific bond durations, and even the price of gold.

Like index mutual funds, ETFs own baskets of stocks and are typically passively managed. ETFs have key advantages over a mutual fund and some clear disadvantages.

First, they are more precise in tracking an index. If you buy an actively managed large-cap stock mutual fund, you may or may not earn the return of the S&P 500, the ultimate large-cap index. That's because you have a manager who is making decisions, and those decisions may not always be right—and the fund could underperform the S&P by a ton. An ETF, meanwhile, is what it is. If it is the iShares MSCI-Japan Index Fund, then it will perform in line with however that Japanese index performs.

Second, ETFs are very tax efficient. As with profits earned from selling shares of stock, you pay taxes on the profits when you sell the ETF—and you have control over when that event takes place because you determine when to sell. With a mutual fund you pay taxes when you sell, but you also get taxed on the dividends the fund distributes to you as well as the capital gains the fund passes on to you when the manager sells stocks that were winners. You have no control over those last two.

Also, the ongoing fees inside an ETF can be less costly, though that's not universally true.

On the downside, if you're the type of investor who uses dollar-cost averaging (discussed earlier in this chapter), ETFs aren't for you because they don't offer direct-investment programs as mutual funds do. Moreover, with an ETF you'll pay a commission for buying and selling, whereas with many mutual funds you don't.

Finally, with an ETF you're not aiming to beat the index since the ETF is designed to match its benchmark. With a good mutual fund, run by a manager with a proven track record, you do have the chance of outperforming the market over the long haul—though most mutual funds do underperform the broader market.

How to Pick a Good Fund: Don't Chase the Hot Ones

Too many investors associate near-term performance with success. But even a blind squirrel is lucky enough to find a nut occasionally, and the same holds for mutual fund managers who luck into a brief period where even the most misguided style of investing works temporarily. The managers and the fund companies that have a long-term record of success are the ones you want to run with.

Mutual funds all post their track records over periods as short as one month and as long as fifteen years or more. "Since inception" tells you how the fund has performed on an annual basis since it opened for business.

Disregard short-term records, those less than three years in length. Short-term numbers tell you nothing except what style of investing has been popular recently. Investors flock to the hottest funds simply because those funds are hot at the moment, and investors wrongly assume past success means future profits. More often than not, the moment in the sun fades, the hot style of investing cools, and investors get burned because they bought in at the top.

Instead, pay attention to the long-term record; it's the most meaningful snapshot of a mutual fund's history. You want to know how a fund performs in good times and bad, over an extended stretch. That way you have an idea of how bad it can get and whether you're comfortable with what could happen. A three-year track record in 2005, for instance, told you nothing about how well a mutual fund held up during the 2000–2002 period, buffeted by the worst bear market in thirty years. Look no further than the Internet sector. Not to pick on a particular fund, but in the three-year period ended in April 2005, the Jacob Internet fund wowed investors with average an-

MORNINGSTAR'S STARS

In mutual fund research, one name stands out: Morningstar.

During the 1990s, as 401(k) plans proliferated, as a mass of individual investors flooded Wall Street, and as the number of mutual funds exploded, a little Chicago-based company, Morningstar, built its reputation as the go-to provider of all sorts of data, research, and commentary on mutual fund performance and management. But it was a bunch of stars that made Morningstar famous.

For each fund the company tracks it assigns a star rating. Five stars—good. One star—not so good. Faced with numerous mutual funds to choose from in their 401(k) plan and thousands more outside of those plans, investors looking for an easy, uncomplicated way to decipher the crush of available data latched onto the star ratings just as they did to brokerage firms' buy, sell, and hold ratings for stocks. The higher the star, they figured, the more Morningstar liked a particular fund.

Yet Morningstar's stars don't actually align that way. The stars are not recommendations to buy or sell a particular mutual fund but are instead symbolic representations of which funds have produced the best and worst returns historically in a given investment style, such as small-cap growth stock funds or medium-term corporate bond funds. In essence, the star ratings judge a mutual fund through the rearview mirror; they don't predict the fund's future course.

Not that that's bad. Knowing that one particular large-company stock fund has performed strongly over a long history while another has lagged the market every year can be a very important variable when considering where to invest your money. You just need to understand the tool before you use it.

Within each mutual fund category, the top 10% of funds earn a five-star rating based on performance over three distinct time periods—three, five, and ten years. Likewise, based on the same objective determinations, the bottom 10% of funds earn just one star. Funds that haven't been around at least three years aren't rated. As even Morningstar notes on its Web site (www.morningstar.com), the stars "shouldn't be considered buy or sell signals."

nual returns of roughly 29% a year, beating the S&P 500 Index by an astounding twenty-five percentage points a year.

Stretch back to the five-year average, however, and all that happiness and light looks like Armageddon. The same fund was down more than 23% a year on average, including losses of 79.1% in 2000 and another 56.4% in 2001.

In short, the short-term numbers mask the truth, so never chase hot funds. Always look back at least five years, or longer if the fund has been around for a while. Some weakness is to be expected in bear markets and sour economies, but the good funds will batten down the hatches and survive intact. One example is the Mairs & Power Growth fund. With its focus on large value- and growth-oriented stocks, the fund purposefully missed the party in the late 1990s when investors tossed aside financial fundamentals to focus on the overhyped promises and the outlandish expectations from new-era technology companies that ultimately failed.

Nevertheless, over its history the Mairs & Power fund has weathered good markets, bad markets, exuberant markets, and dull markets. For its efforts it ranks among the top 1% of all mutual funds over ten and fifteen years, piling up returns of 15.1% annually, much better than the S&P 500. The fund also stands out as one of the single best during the bear market. As a long-term investor, that's the kind of mutual fund you want to wake up with each morning.

Ultimately, owning stocks, bonds, and mutual funds comes down to this: As long as you don't chase hot funds and hot stock tips, as long as you don't try to time the market, and as long as you rebalance your account annually, a balanced mix of assets that makes you comfortable will do just fine over time.

ASSET ALLOCATION

The academics who study Wall Street have shown that more than 90% of a portfolio's overall long-term success depends not on what you own but how you allocate your money.

That means the mix of assets you own—the assortment of stocks, bonds, cash, real estate, etc., that comprise your portfolio—means more to your success than do the individual investments.

That mix is what Wall Street pros call an asset allocation. Though figuring out how much of this and how much of that you need in your portfolio might seem intimidating, particularly when you have thousands upon thousands of stocks, bonds, and mutual funds to choose from, the reality is that asset allocation isn't very difficult at all. Too many people, however, operate on the extremes: They either invest all their money in high-growth stocks, hoping to shoot the lights out, or they're overly protective of their nest egg and stick it entirely in bonds or cash. Neither approach is particularly wise. A portfolio overloaded with stocks faces the risks inherent in a broad-based bear market that can eradicate a large share of your money. Too much in bonds or cash, however, leaves you vulnerable to inflation and the risk that your money doesn't grow nearly fast enough to meet your needs later in life.

This is where asset allocation comes in. Different classes of assets—stocks, bonds, gold, real estate—move in different ways and generally not in unison. Stocks, for instance, typically move based on corporate earnings and the outlook for the overall economy; bonds usually move with interest rates; gold moves on geopolitical tensions and currency woes; oil moves on waxing and waning fears of supply shortages and the ebb and flow of global energy demands. A properly allocated portfolio means you own a mix of these different assets so that when one asset is moving down, another is likely moving up, counterbalancing your risk.

The basic rule is this: The younger you are, the more money you should allocate to stocks. The older you grow, the more you increase your exposure to bonds.

The rationale: Younger workers need in their earlier years the growth that stocks provide, while older savers need the safety of high-grade corporate and government bonds to preserve their nest egg. If the stock market tanks when you're younger, the losses will sting, but you still have many years to rebuild your account. Investing too much in bonds early on, however, means you risk not earning enough of a return through the years to accumulate an adequately sized retirement account.

Conversely, if you're older and nearing retirement when the stock market tanks (or, worse, you're in retirement), you won't have nearly enough time to replenish what was lost. That will crimp your lifestyle. Thus, putting increasing amounts of your portfolio into bonds as you age protects you from just such a disaster, since the price of high-quality federal, municipal, and corporate bonds doesn't fall that far, even in a rotten year.

Now, when Wall Street professionals talk about asset allocation, you often hear them talking in terms of "allocation model," or the percentage of your total portfolio allocated to various classes of investments. The most generic asset allocation model is the so-called 60-40 split, in which 60% of your dollars go into the stock market while 40% goes into the bond market. You lie awake at night worried about this portfolio because you get reasonable growth from the stocks yet consistent income and a buffer against volatility by way of the bonds. The stock component is often invested in an S&P 500 Index fund, such as the ones offered by Fidelity and Vanguard, both of which are ultra-low cost. The bond component, meanwhile, is typically in U.S. Treasury bonds, the safest bond investment in the world, given that the money is backed by the full faith and credit of the U.S. government. Some investors use municipal bonds or high-grade corporate bonds, both of which can provide slightly beefier returns with only marginally more risk.

For a slightly more personalized approach, a widely used rule of thumb suggests you subtract your age from 100—or 120, for more aggressive investors—and stick that percentage of your portfolio in stocks. The remainder goes into bonds. A thirty-five-year-old, for instance, would stick between 65% and 85% of a portfolio in stocks, with the remainder aimed at bonds. In formula terms it looks like this:

$$\text{\% in Stocks} = 100 \text{ (or } 120) - \text{Current Age}$$
$$\underline{\hspace{2cm}} = 100 \text{ (or } 120) - \underline{\hspace{2cm}}$$

This approach is much more sensitive to your working career, since it ensures that as you age you automatically scale back your stock exposure and increase your bond holdings. Plus, it always keeps you in stocks to some degree—well, unless you live past 120. Even in old age—meaning people into their seventies and even eighties—retaining a bit of stock market exposure is important. Stocks provide the fuel necessary to keep your money growing faster than inflation, since you never know how long you'll need to draw upon your cash in retirement.

Once you determine how the cash in your portfolio should be divided, then comes the big question: What to buy? The cheat sheet below can help determine that answer. Know, though, that this cheat sheet is aimed at folks saving largely through mutual funds in a retirement-savings plan such as a 401(k). You can adapt it for various IRAs or even a standard brokerage account. And although you can apply the general principles to individual stocks and bonds and such, this cheat sheet isn't really designed for that.

- If you have access to an S&P 500 Index fund, that's where you want the bulk of your stock market allocation. All 401(k) plans generally have one of these. If you own no other stock market exposure, a fund that shadows the S&P 500 will serve you well over time, since over the long term the U.S. stock market trends upward. Plus, the internal fees with index funds are some of the lowest in the mutual fund world. If your plan does not offer an S&P 500 fund or some similar broad-market fund, then go with a large-company stock fund that has a track record of decent returns over the last five years at the very least.

- Put a small percentage in small-company stocks. Historically, this has been a top-performing fund class over long periods. But you don't want to overdo it: Small-company stocks are very aggressive and risky, since small companies not only grow fast, they implode fast. You might find in your 401(k) plan a small-cap index fund that tracks the Russell 2000; that's the best bet. If not, you'll probably have a single, actively managed small-cap fund as your only choice. Beggars can't be choosers.

- Venture abroad. Most 401(k) plans offer an international fund of some sort. Put a small portion (no more than 20%) of your stock market allocation into international stocks. They are risky and volatile. But they actually improve the overall stability of your portfolio and enhance the returns. That's because the U.S. market is rarely the best performing one in the world; in any given year, any of numerous other markets around the globe claim that distinction. Plus, owning just American companies limits your growth prospects because the world is filled with very good, very profitable companies that do not trade on the New York Stock Exchange. Some 401(k) plans will offer a variety of international index funds; some will offer actively managed funds. In this instance, actively managed funds are often better. International index funds typically own the biggest companies in a particular country; that's fine, but many of those companies have economic ties in some fashion to the U.S. marketplace. Good international-fund managers are better at looking past the obvious, large companies and finding the solid, smaller local companies responsible for much of a country's underlying growth that aren't tied to U.S. consumers in any real way.

- Buy a real estate investment trust, a REIT. Not all 401(k) plans offer such an option, though the numbers are increasing. Statistically, real estate provides a counterbalance in a portfolio since it has very little correlation to the movements of the stock and bond market. That means real estate largely moves independently of stocks and bonds, providing added diversification to a portfolio. All you need is 5% of your overall portfolio in REIT shares and you're fine.

- Own an intermediate-term bond-index fund, if your plan offers one. These are funds that own bonds with maturities of between four and ten years; they're often in the sweet spot of the bond market. If your plan doesn't offer a bond-index fund, then go with the bond fund that has an "average duration" in the five- to seven-year range, or something close to that. You can find that average duration number in the fund's prospectus, though going to Morningstar.com, plugging in the fund's five-letter ticker symbol, and reading about the details on the "Snapshot" page is far easier.

- Go with a TIPS fund if you have access to one. TIPS stands for Treasury Inflation Protected Securities, U.S. government securities designed to provide a return that always beats inflation. You can't go wrong staying ahead of inflation, since it means your dollars are growing faster than the price of bread at the corner market.

- Skip sector funds. Individual investors often gravitate to funds that specialize in one corner of Wall Street, particularly technology, hoping to score a big return. They often wind up getting burned instead because sector funds tend to be more volatile and aggressive—basically, risky—than are plain-vanilla, broad-based mutual funds. There's no reason to gamble with your future simply to try to squeeze a marginal bit of additional return from your portfolio by taking on substantially more risk.

- Finally, if you don't want the hassle of trying to figure out any of this, stick your entire 401(k) balance in a life cycle fund, a mutual fund built to be a one-stop shop for investors who don't want to have to think about owning anything other than a single investment. Life cycle funds have targeted maturity dates as much as thirty to forty years into the future. They're built to change with you as you age, growing increasingly risk-averse as you grow older and the targeted maturity date draws nearer. Equally important: You aren't likely to rack up big losses since the funds are diversified across different types of investments. These funds are growing increasingly popular in retirement plans, because with one investment decision, you're adequately diversified and properly allocated instantly based on your age—now and throughout the future.

CHAPTER 5

PLANNING

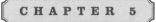

Financial success doesn't happen without a little planning—and planning to win the lottery doesn't count.

A child's college tuition. Your retirement. A new car. A first house. A vacation home. That blowout holiday you've been dreaming about for years. All of these big expenses and many more don't just happen by sprinkling a little pixie dust. You have to plan for what you want so that you can map the route to your goal. Certainly winning the lottery is more convenient, but determining to save the necessary funds over time on your own is more sensible.

With patience you can reach any realistic aim you can envision, though you must accept that success doesn't happen overnight.

In this chapter we're going to concentrate on planning for two of the biggest financial costs you're likely to confront in life: (1) saving for retirement and investing the assets so that you don't have to worry about your nest egg constantly, and (2) saving money for college and finding the resources to help lessen your out-of-pocket costs. Statistically speaking, you'll have a good fifteen to twenty years in retirement, and unless you can happily subsist on Social Security income—assuming it's still available when you retire—you'll need to have saved several hundred thousand dollars by the time you quit working.

College will be cheaper since it lasts far fewer years, yet

it still promises to be one of the most expensive price tags, cumulatively, you'll ever pay. Of course you don't necessarily have to pay the full freight for a child's education. Many parents want their kids to earn part of their college cost by working their way through school, and some want their kids to take on a reasonable amount of debt they must pay off after school so that they will better appreciate the cost of their degree.

If you have the resources to fund only one major expense, then retirement saving is your best option. That might sound heartless, but your financial self-sufficiency in old age may be the best gift you ever give your kids because there's a very good chance they'd rather pay down their own college debt than have a mom and dad continually seeking assistance with monthly bills.

The fact is, college can be financed and the debt paid off over your child's working career. Your child can find grants and scholarships or work his way through school. Retirement, however, cannot be financed. No one offers grants for you to retire, and it's a safe bet that after working your entire life you're not going to want to work your way through retirement. Combined, the cash, investments, Social Security, and pension income you retire with create the only paycheck you'll have to live on for possibly decades. For that reason, preparing adequately for your golden years is much more important to your finances than saving for your child's college.

If you can afford to do both, that's great. And if you learn to better manage your income and your outflow, then you just might be in a position to fund both a retirement and a college account. Either way, success starts with knowing where you are now and plotting a map to get you to where you want to go. That starts with your net worth.

NET WORTH

Your total assets minus your total liabilities is your net worth. This marks the first step toward your future—knowing what defines your present. If you don't know where you are, then getting to where you want to go hinges on a hope that you're moving in the right direction. And hope is never a solid financial foundation.

Tally up the value of every asset you own, everything from the current market value of your car to investments, a house and furnishings, and that vintage collection of Richie Rich comic books in Mom's attic. Subtract from that all the debt you owe for everything from college loans to a mortgage, a car note, and your credit-card balance. This tells you exactly how much cash would remain if you sold every possession and paid off every obligation. Don't trick yourself by overvaluing some hard-to-price asset—such as those vintage comics. The market value for obscure assets is rarely as high as we like to imagine. ✎ *page 119*

By itself your net worth is just a number that doesn't really do much; it's static, like a photograph. It's not interactive like your budget, which you can monkey with to gauge how added income or altered spending changes your daily finances. If you monkey with your net worth, you're just playing a game of wishful thinking since your net worth is simply a reflection of the reality of your life. If you own $100 and you owe $50, well, neither number is open to interpretation.

Knowing your net worth is important, however, if only for one reason: It forces you to interact with your financial life, keeping you in touch with your money and knowledgeable about where you are on the road to where you think you're going.

How often should you calculate your net worth? At least annually, so that you see the regular signposts of progress and feel as though you are moving toward your goals. If you share life with a partner whose only relationship with the family's finances is the checkbook or ATM card, you might consider calculating the family's net worth more frequently, either quarterly or semiannually, so that your partner has the same sense of progress you do and can feel clued into and comfortable with the family's financial situation.

Once you know your net worth, you can begin mapping your future.

RETIREMENT PLANNING

Why, you might think, would you save for retirement before you save for a child's education? After all, educational costs will arrive first, and you'll then have a number of years afterward to accumulate money to live on in retirement.

Quite simply it is because, as expensive as college costs promise to be, retirement promises to make college seem like little more than a pricey dinner at a fancy eatery. Statistically, if you reach sixty-five, you can expect to live another fifteen to twenty years—and that life expectancy keeps extending alongside health care advances. Meanwhile, the oldest Americans— those in their eighties and nineties—are the fastest-growing segment of the population.

The nut of all this is that you're likely to have many, many years to finance in retirement, and Social Security is designed to cover only about 40% of your retirement income. Each year near their birthday eligible workers receive from the Social Security Administration a statement of their expected Social Security benefits, giving them a good idea of how much extra they'll need to generate in order to live at the standard of living they'd like. If you have never looked at these statements and don't have one lying around, you can request a copy online at www.socialsecurity.gov. You can also gauge your estimated benefits online or download a more detailed calculator at www.socialsecurity.gov/planners/calculators.htm.

How Social Security might operate when you retire is anyone's guess, but chances are that it will still be around in some form, maybe even the current form, to provide you with some income. Here is what that income looked like in 2005, based on various levels of earnings. Note, for instance, that if you retired today earning $50,000, you'd get $14,628 annually from

Social Security. If you happen to be in the 25% tax bracket, that means Social Security is covering roughly 40% of your take-home pay.

WHAT WILL I GET FROM SOCIAL SECURITY?	
Annual Earnings	Approximate Monthly Benefit (based on 2005 data)
$ 10,000	$ 486
20,000	699
30,000	872
40,000	1,046
50,000	1,219
60,000	1,392
70,000	1,544
80,000	1,626
90,000	1,706
100,000	1,778
110,000	1,828
120,000	1,860
130,000	1,873
140,000 or more	1,874

Whatever Social Security doesn't cover must come from your own pocket. Unlike college costs, which can be financed by you or your kids, retirement is pay as you go. What makes retirement planning so confounding is that the amount you'll ultimately need is impossible to know since you have no clue how long you'll live, how healthy you'll be, or what you might decide you want to do and where you want to do it decades from now. Even the online retirement-planning calculators aren't much help. Plug in the same data, and you get wildly varying results telling you how much you need to save today to end up where you want to be tomorrow.

The ultimate goal in saving for retirement isn't to accumulate a specific dollar amount, it's saving consistently through the years as much as you comfortably can, living within your means along the way, and then living within your means once you've retired. Studies have shown that the most content re-tirees are those who planned and saved the longest. They might not have accumulated the most assets, but they reached retirement knowing they saved prudently throughout their life and that they can live within the bounds of what they have. Those who are most fearful of not having enough are those who satisfied their urge to spend over the years and saved for the shortest amount of time.

In the roughest of terms, you will need anywhere from 70% to more than 100% of your annual working-life income to live in retirement as well as you do today. If you're close to retirement—within a few years—you have a fairly good notion of how much income you need to live on; this makes it a bit easier to gauge what retirement will cost on a yearly basis. If you're still decades away, then your estimate is no better than a crapshoot. In the companion workbook to this guide you'll find a retirement planning worksheet to help you at least ap-proximate your savings needs for retirement. ✎ *page 147*

Certainly there are lots of expenses you'll no longer have when you retire, such as commuting costs, new business attire, workday meals outside the office, and retirement plan contri-butions, to name a few. With luck you won't still be paying for your kids and your home will be paid off, axing big monthly expenses. Yet interviews with retirees have shown that you typ-ically add in retirement lots of expenses you didn't think about: additional health care costs in the form of an increased number of visits to various doctors as you age, the cost of phar-maceuticals you may not have needed when you were younger, and increased health insurance premiums and co-pays as com-panies continue to scale back their health coverage for re-tirees. You may decide you want to travel more in retirement; you may want to live out your days in a nicer house or drive a nicer car or fish from a nicer bass boat; or you may want to help your grandchildren pay for educational costs. Perhaps you'll pick up an expensive hobby such as scuba diving or rais-ing horses.

Whatever the reason, retirement is almost always pricier than most folks imagine. So let's get started planning for the inevitable.

THE 401(K)

You can't spell retirement without 401(k). Since its introduction in 1982, the now ubiquitous 401(k) plan has become a staple of employees' lives and has effectively replaced pension plans that workers once relied on for retirement income.

These retirement savings plans are named for the section of the federal tax code—section 401, paragraph (k)—that gives them their tax-advantaged status. That advantage is this: You're allowed to save money that comes out of your paycheck *before* the Internal Revenue Service imposes taxes on your income. Moreover, those contributions and all the money they subsequently earn grows tax-deferred until you start to withdraw the funds in retirement.

However, just because you're investing $1 in a 401(k) plan doesn't mean your paycheck shrinks by $1. Because you're doing this before Uncle Sam takes his cut, you're reducing your taxable income and, thus, the amount of taxes you owe. In a simple example, suppose you earn $1,000 a week and pay 25% in taxes. Prior to joining a 401(k) plan, your paycheck loses $250 to taxes, and you take home $750. After signing up to save, say, 5% of your salary, your employer will subtract from your paycheck $50 ($1,000 × 0.05) to put into your 401(k) account before calculating taxes on the remaining $950. In this case you now owe the government $237.50 in taxes ($950 × 0.25), meaning your take-home pay is $712.50. Essentially, you saved $50 for retirement, but your paycheck is only $37.50 lighter.

Note: Tax-deferred does not mean tax-free. Tax-free means you pay no taxes ever. Tax-deferred means you'll owe taxes at a later date, generally once you withdraw the money. At that point you'll pay taxes on both the profits you amass as well as your original contributions. Since those original dollars weren't taxed on the way in, the IRS taxes them on the way out.

In addition, the taxes owed will be based on whatever your prevailing ordinary income rate is at the time of withdrawal, not the capital-gains rate at which most investments are taxed. Ordinary income rates are typically higher than capital gains rates, though that hasn't always been the case historically and may not always be the case in the future. The assumption is that your ordinary income rate, which moves up and down based on the size of your income, will be lower in retirement than it was during your working career because your income is often lower once you pack away the lunch pail for good.

One of the great attributes of a 401(k) plan is that employers often kick in a contribution, too, though that's not universally true. Typically, employers contribute between 25 cents and $1 for every $1 you save, up to a certain amount. Sometimes that amount is just 1% of your salary, but it could be 5% or more. Whatever the case, this is free money. Think about it this way: If you saw in the newspaper that a local bank was offering to add an extra 50 cents to every dollar a customer deposits, how long do you think the line would stretch for people waiting to open that account? A 401(k) is the same concept.

Of course there is a catch: Once you start contributing, you can't touch the money until you're 59½. If you do, then the IRS hits you up for taxes on the amount of money you withdraw plus a 10% penalty.

CHANGING JOBS

If you leave your employer, you can take your account with you—a characteristic known as "portability." In many cases you can also leave the money with your former employer or roll the cash into an IRA (more on that in a moment).

The most efficient, financially savvy option for workers is to request that your former employer transfer the money directly into your new employer's retirement plan, assuming your new employer offers one, or into an IRA that you set up through a brokerage firm or mutual fund company.

If you request a check for the balance of your 401(k) account, you have just sixty days to deposit that money into another 401(k) plan or a rollover IRA. If you don't, the entire amount is hit with taxes and penalties. Moreover, when you take a distribution upon leaving your job, your former employer is required to withhold 20% for tax purposes. That means you'll ultimately need to come up with that missing 20% so that the balance you deposit into a new account exactly matches what was in the old account.

If your account balance is more than $5,000 when you change jobs, you have the right to leave your money in your former employer's 401(k) plan. You won't be making additional contributions, however, nor will your former employer, though the account will grow alongside whatever investment options you have selected.

The worst option is taking the distribution and keeping the money. The taxes and penalties will consume at least 30% of the account balance and rob you of substantially more income at retirement since this money is not in the market working for you.

VESTING

Employers generally impose a vesting schedule on workers, giving them access each year to a larger portion of the employer's contribution but not the entire amount. At the end of year one, for instance, you might have access to only 20% or 25% of what your employer kicked in if you decide to leave for another job. At the end of year two, you might get to take with you between 40% and 50%. All the money you put into the plan is 100% yours from day one.

Companies are increasingly offering workers immediate vesting, meaning that from the very first contribution all money in the account—yours and whatever the company contributes—belongs to you entirely.

Post-tax 401(k) Contributions

Though not often used this way, 401(k) plans also allow workers to make after-tax contributions. The benefit of saving after-tax dollars is that if you need the money early, you can withdraw your contributions tax-free since they were taxed going in. You cannot withdraw any gains tax-free, however. In addition, any contributions your employer makes cannot be withdrawn until age 59½ unless you want to pay the tax and penalties. The drawback of post-tax saving is a smaller paycheck since you're not only taxed on the full amount of your income but are subtracting a retirement contribution on top of that. In the example above, after paying taxes on your $1,000 salary, you have $750 remaining, and then you take away the $50 contribution, leaving you with $700 in net pay.

The 401(k) and Bankruptcy . . . or Corporate Fraud

With all the shenanigans that tainted Wall Street in the early part of this decade (Enron, WorldCom, Adelphia) workers are rightly concerned about a corporate implosion. While you might rightfully worry about where your next paycheck will come from, your 401(k) is protected. Under the federal Employee Retirement Income Security Act (routinely referred to as ERISA in the financial world), 401(k) assets are held in trust in a separate account just for you. Once the money is in that account, your company cannot touch it for any purposes related to maintaining the business.

Company Stock

Many public companies pay their portion of 401(k) contributions in company stock, and many workers buy additional shares, either in their 401(k) account or through a stock purchase plan. Beware.

Enron investors learned the hard way just how sour owning company stock can be. One of the basic rules of financial planning is not to put too many of your assets in one investment—the old "don't keep all your eggs in one basket" rule of money management. Think about it this way: Your livelihood is already dependent on your company in the form of your paycheck. There's no reason to hitch another key part of your financial life—your retirement plan—to your company as well. A good rule is to hold no more than 10% of your overall portfolio in company stock.

How Much to Save?

At the very least save 1%. Companies generally require workers to save in full percentage point increments, so 1% is the smallest contribution you can make. More important, that 1% will help instill a savings ethic that, over time, will translate into a nice cushion of cash.

If you can swing it, save up to the amount your company will match. If your company offers to pay you 50 cents for every dollar you save up to the first 5% of your salary, then try to save at least 5% of your salary. Remember: This is free money. Don't let it slip away. If you earn $40,000 a year and save $2,000 (5%), then a $1,000 company match is the equivalent of a 2.5% pay raise—only it goes directly into your retirement savings instead of your wallet.

That 2.5% might seem small, but over many paychecks over many years, small percentages add up to very large dollars.

Don't fret, though, if you can't quite muster the company

THE ALPHANUMERIC RETIREMENT SOUP

Although it is one of the most widely owned retirement saving accounts, the 401(k) isn't alone. Companies, non-profit organizations, and government agencies operate a variety of other retirement plans, including the 401(a), 403(a), 403(b), 457, and Thrift Savings Plan.

All have their individual quirks, but essentially they each provide you with a similar benefit—namely, the opportunity to save part of your salary in an account that grows tax-deferred until retirement.

With some, such as the 401(a) plans, pre-tax employee contributions are not allowed. Others are designed for a particular kind of company. For instance, 403(b) plans are the exclusive province of workers at tax-exempt organizations such as public schools and colleges, teaching hospitals, and charitable organizations. State and local government workers save in 457 plans, while federal civilian employees and members of the uniformed military save in the Thrift Savings Plan.

match at first. Save the minimum 1% and then commit to increasing that percentage by one percentage point every six months or, at the very least, every year. In addition, if you receive an annual bonus, plow half into your 401(k) plan. That way you get the benefit of enjoying more discretionary income, yet you're also saving more for your future. Before you know it, you'll be saving the maximum the IRS allows.

WHAT ARE THE MAXIMUMS?

IRS rules limit how much money a worker can stash annually into a 401(k) account. That amount in 2006 is $15,000. Starting in 2007 the annual limit increases by $500 per year to help savers keep up with inflation.

Congress, worried about a crush of financially ill-prepared baby boomers rushing toward retirement, has given that group a special "catch-up provision" that allows them to save more. In 2006, boomers aged fifty and above can save an extra $5,000 a year for a total of $20,000. Like the standard contributions, the catch-up provision will rise by $500 each year thereafter, meaning the provision will allow an additional contribution of $5,500 in 2007.

Where to Invest:
The Mass of 401(k) Options

In the early days of the 401(k), investors often had very limited options, sometimes just a money-market account or a bond fund. Today, in some plans, workers have the entire world of stocks, bonds, and mutual funds available to them—an option known as a brokerage window because it allows workers to trade through a brokerage firm affiliated with the plan.

By and large most companies realize that too many options is, well, too many options for workers to digest. As a result, most plans offer employees between fifteen and twenty mutual funds; typically they include domestic and foreign stock funds; short- and medium-term U.S. government bond funds; and index funds focused on either small-, mid-, or large-cap stocks, or a broad-market index such as the Standard & Poor's 500.

Increasingly, plans are including so-called lifestyle funds that aim for a targeted maturity date sometime in the future. These are one-stop asset-allocation funds that leave the decisions on what proportion of assets to own to the pros who make their living at managing money. So instead of worrying about allocating her own assets, our pizza-parlor owner—let's assume she's forty years old and wants to retire in twenty years—could invest in a lifestyle fund set to mature roughly around her retirement date, say in 2025. The managers of that

REBALANCING IN JUST THIRTY MINUTES A YEAR: THE ART OF TIMING

Rebalancing a portfolio means seeking that optimum spot where you're comfortable with the risk you're taking, yet you're also seeking as much return as possible.

At some point during the year you match what you currently have in your account against your predetermined asset allocation, covered in the Investing section. That's it.

In rebalancing your account, you pare back what has grown too plump and plump up what has withered. By doing this you are by definition selling into the strength of your best-performing investments and buying into the weakness of the laggards. In short, you're buying low and selling high—the very mantra that Wall Street lives by.

To rebalance, all you do is calculate what percentage each asset represents in your portfolio currently, and then figure out how much you need to sell or buy of that particular asset to get it back in line with where it should be according to your personal asset allocation needs.

For example, say you've determined you should have 65% in stocks and 35% in bonds, yet after a rollicking year for the stock market, you see that your portfolio now has 74% in stocks and just 26% in bonds. In this case you sell 9% of your stocks and use that cash to increase your bond investments. And, voilà, you're rebalanced.

Don't try to rebalance to take advantage of trends at the moment. If you feel that the bond market is due for a tumble because interest rates are rising, the scenario that played out in 2005, don't try to overcompensate by selling down your bond portfolio for a greater exposure to stocks or some other asset. In doing so you'd be trying to time the market, a generally losing strategy. Market timing, by necessity, is a two-trade transaction. You might be lucky enough to get in or out at the perfect moment, but will you be lucky enough to know when to pull the trigger on the reverse trade? And are you smart enough to do that time and time again? Statistically you're not since mounds of research show that market timers underperform simple buy-and-hold investing. Stick to your asset allocation, and you'll have a worry-free portfolio tailored to your needs.

Otherwise you'll spend too much time wondering if today is the day to switch back into bonds . . . or was it yesterday?

How often you rebalance is a personal decision based on your desire to dig into your investments on a regular basis. Some people do it every quarter; some get around to it whenever they remember, maybe every few years. Some never do it.

Rebalancing too frequently accumulates excessive trading costs, thereby trimming your returns. Plus, if you're constantly jiggering the portfolio, your investments don't have time to work for you. Don't rebalance enough, though, and you risk letting one portion of your portfolio grow too fat, thereby subjecting yourself to the risk that a blowup in that part of the market will hit your portfolio particularly hard. That is what pinched so many individual investors when the technology bubble burst in 2000. People who let their technology exposure balloon felt a real sting when the pop came.

In general you want to rebalance about once a year, maybe in late December as the year ends or early January as the new one begins. It will keep your portfolio in tune with your progression toward retirement, it will keep your asset mix consistent with your needs, and it will keep you adequately involved in your investments without making them a burden.

It will take all of thirty minutes.

fund would invest more aggressively in the early years since they have two decades to grow the assets and plenty of time to compensate for market downdrafts along the way. But as the years pass, the managers will increasingly reallocate the portfolio into safer investments so that our pizza maven won't risk losing her nest egg if the stock market crashes on the Tuesday before she retires.

Some 401(k) plans also now include a real-estate investment trust, a so-called REIT, and maybe even a gold fund. While both of these can be risky on their own, as a small part of a portfolio—generally no more than about 5% of a portfolio's total value—they can actually reduce the overall risk and enhance the return slightly. They accomplish this because movements in the price of real estate and gold have historically had a very low correlation with the price movement of stocks and bonds, meaning they don't move in tandem. Thus, they provide increased diversification and balance to your asset mix.

The asset allocation you ultimately work up for yourself will help determine which investments you should own. When it comes to actually choosing between various mutual funds in your plan, Web sites such as www.morningstar.com, which tracks mutual fund performance and other key information, can be invaluable. The free portion of that site provides an abundance of easily digested data on thousands of funds. The paid site offers substantially more in terms of research and analysis.

Also, if you have access to a brokerage window, it's best to skip that and stick to the mutual funds. Unless you have the time and inclination to analyze, choose, and watch over individual stocks and bonds, it's easier to let the pros worry about the individual investments. Plus, brokerage windows are generally more expensive because you have to pay the commissions each time you buy and sell. With mutual funds inside your 401(k) you typically don't.

THE 401(k) LOAN: A BORROWER AND LENDER ALL IN ONE

What would Polonius think? He in *Hamlet* who admonished his son, Laertes, "Neither a borrower, nor a lender be" would likely not know what to make of a 401(k) loan. After all, with one transaction you manage to be both borrower and lender at the same time.

You borrow from the savings you've accumulated, and in doing so you're lending to yourself. Many workers like this option because, they figure, "How can I go wrong if I'm paying myself back with interest instead of repaying a bank?"

That sounds logical enough, and there is some benefit to that if you fully understand what you're doing. Yet there are also misconceptions, caveats, and risks associated with a 401(k) loan. First, there's the word *loan* itself. It's a misnomer. You're not really "borrowing" the money. You're actually selling off a part of your account and taking a partial withdrawal. It's not as if the money in your account remains invested in stocks and bonds and continues to grow. No, the money you've "borrowed" is no longer at work for you in investment markets. Instead, it is pulled from your account and grows at a rate equivalent to the interest rate you're charged on the loan.

The IRS agrees to forgive any taxes and penalties you would otherwise owe on a partial withdrawal as long as you promise to repay the loan. At most companies that usually means repaying the balance over no more than five years, though you'll have up to fifteen or twenty years if you use the loan to buy your first home. Companies typically require that you repay through payroll deductions, meaning the money comes out of your paycheck—after taxes—before you get your hands on it. If you don't repay the loan, the IRS taxes the outstanding balance at whatever your current income tax rate is, and it imposes a 10% penalty on top of that.

But let's back up a minute. While most 401(k) plans allow for loans, not all do. If a company does allow 401(k) loans, then a plan participant—that's you—can borrow up to $50,000, or one-half of the value of the account, whichever is smaller. You can borrow for any reason—good or bad—be it that first home purchase, to buy a car or a boat, or to splurge on a month-long tour of America's roadside museums.

The interest rate is usually set at a percentage point or two above the so-called prime rate—the rate that banks charge their most credit-worthy commercial customers. Thus, in early 2005 when the prime rate was 5.5%, many 401(k) loans charged about 6.5% or so. Aside from determining your repayment amount, that rate also marks the absolute limit your borrowed money can grow since the cash is no longer invested in stock and bond mutual funds. While that was certainly a decent rate of return at a time when the broader stock market was down for the year, you have to keep in mind that the loan will likely stretch over several years, subjecting you to the possibility that you'll miss the more normalized stock market returns of between 9% and 11% a year. If your loan is large enough—say 50% of your account balance—and you use it to buy a home or routinely raid your account for consumer wants, then that rate can diminish the amount of money you'd otherwise have at retirement.

Moreover, you're repaying the loan with after-tax dollars, not pre-tax dollars, so that money is not tax advantaged. And when you start to draw down the account in retirement, you'll pay taxes again on that money. In essence, you're paying taxes twice on the same dollars.

Then there's this risk to consider: if you're fired, laid off, or resign while you have a loan balance still outstanding. In that event you generally have thirty to sixty days to fully repay what you still owe. If you can't muster up the necessary cash, the IRS will tax and penalize the remaining balance. Chances are that if you had to borrow from your 401(k) in the first place because you couldn't scrounge up the necessary funds elsewhere, then it would be tougher still to amass the cash needed to repay the loan balance before the IRS comes calling.

401(k) HARDSHIP WITHDRAWAL

Aside from a loan, the IRS allows workers with demonstrated financial need to take a hardship withdrawal. This is different from a 401(k) loan in that you don't repay the money. You will pay taxes on the amount withdrawn, however, as well as a 10% penalty if you're under 59½. Don't discount that bite. Say you need $10,000 for whatever reason. If you're in the 27% tax bracket, you must withdraw $15,873 to end up with the money you need and pay the tax along with the penalty.

The IRS allows hardship withdrawals for just a limited

number of reasons: (1) to pay twelve months of educational expenses for you, a spouse, or a child, (2) to prevent being evicted from your home, (3) to buy a home if you're a first-time home owner, and (4) to pay unreimbursed medical expenses. As of January 1, 2006, you're permitted to take a hardship withdrawal to pay funeral costs for an immediate family member or to repair damage caused to your primary residence by a natural disaster.

Moreover, if you take a hardship withdrawal, the IRS reckons your finances are so tight that you shouldn't be using your money for anything other than pressing financial needs. As such, you will not be allowed to contribute to your 401(k) for six months—nor will your company kick in its matching contribution during that time.

The upshot is that your account's ability to provide for you in retirement, when you need it most, will be severely weakened.

ROTH 401(k) PLANS

These plans, effective January 1, 2006, are a cross between a traditional 401(k) plan and a Roth IRA. Essentially you're allowed to save money from your paycheck, as with a traditional 401(k) plan, but the money comes out after taxes, not pre-tax like with the traditional setup. Then, like with a Roth IRA, those contributions and the earnings they generate compound tax-free, meaning you can ultimately withdraw them in retirement without paying any taxes.

That sounds like a winning proposition, and for many workers it is. But a Roth 401(k) isn't for everyone. The big question you must determine—and it's a doozy—is what tax bracket you're likely to fall into in retirement. That's a challenge for most people, since it's so hard to guess what your income will be through the years and the size your nest egg might ultimately reach. Nevertheless, workers who expect to be in a lower tax bracket in retirement than they are now are generally ill-suited for a Roth 401(k). The reason: You get a bigger tax break by saving pre-tax dollars today while you're in a higher tax bracket, and then paying taxes at a lower rate on your traditional 401(k) withdrawals later in retirement.

Conversely, workers who know they will be in a higher tax bracket—essentially those who already have or expect to have a large nest egg that will generate substantial income in retirement—are likely to benefit from a Roth 401(k). They'll get a bigger break by paying taxes at a lower rate now than by waiting to pay a higher tax rate they'd face with traditional 401(k) distributions later.

Three other groups of workers should consider a Roth 401(k) as well:

1. Young workers, those just starting out, should almost *always* invest in a Roth 401(k) over a traditional 401(k). Their contributions and profits will compound over decades, potentially massing into a sum of tax-free money much larger than they'd receive from a same-sized investment in a traditional 401(k) plan. That's because while the two pots of money would grow to an identical size, the traditional 401(k) would impose taxes on all the profits and contributions on the way out. The Roth, meanwhile, would tax only the contributions on the way in. All the profits—likely to be the bulk of the account in retirement—would come out tax-free.

The downside for young workers is that their paychecks will be smaller with a Roth 401(k), a side effect many lower-paid young workers might not stomach when they're already scrounging for every dollar. Remember that contributions to a traditional 401(k) reduce your income before taxes are deducted, thereby shrinking your tax bite. With a Roth, you're taxed on your full income—meaning a larger tax obligation. Only then is your 401(k) contribution deducted from your after-tax pay. Consider this very simplistic example: A single person earning $1,000 a week, paying taxes at 25%, and wanting to save $100 each week in a 401(k). With the traditional 401(k), the $100 is deducted first, meaning the 25% tax obligation is imposed on the remaining $900. The result is a paycheck of $675.

With the Roth, the 25% taxes are taken out first, leaving $750. Only then is the $100 deducted, leaving you with a paycheck of $650—$25 less than with the traditional 401(k).

2. Parents—or grandparents—saving for college who have at least five years to go before a child enrolls, and who will be at least 59½ when that happens, should look to a Roth 401(k) regardless of income or their future tax situation.

When college arrives, those savers can pull money from these accounts tax-free to help pay the bills. What's ultimately left remains in your name, not in the child's name, and, as with a 529 college savings plan, doesn't have to be used for educational expenses. Moreover, money in retirement accounts such as a 401(k) plan generally isn't counted as assets in the federal financial aid formulas, potentially helping a student obtain a larger slug of financial aid, but more on that in the college-planning area coming up shortly.

3. Finally, a Roth can provide a novel estate-planning option for retirees who expect to have plenty to live on from other sources of income. Unlike traditional 401(k)s, Roth 401(k)s don't mandate that a certain amount of money begin to be distributed by age 70½, what's known as "required minimum distributions." That feature could turn the Roth 401(k) into a vehicle for passing wealth to heirs tax efficiently.

Before you choose between a Roth and traditional 401(k) plan, talk to a tax pro about your specific situation, since being in the wrong plan can cost you a lot of missed income in retirement.

INDIVIDUAL RETIREMENT ACCOUNTS

IRAs, as these are called, are similar to 401(k)s in that they are generally tax-deferred retirement savings accounts. One key distinction is that you're not pulling pre-tax dollars out of each paycheck to fund an IRA. The money you plow into an IRA comes from dollars that have already been taxed.

Along with the tax-deferred growth of your contributions and their earnings, the federal government gives you another incentive to contribute: a tax deduction every year on the money you put into an IRA if you meet certain qualifications. Once you start wading through all the qualifications and numerous permutations that are possible, however, it begins to read like this: If you're married and it's the first Tuesday after a harvest moon and you have a blue-eyed sister who is single with three cats . . . In short, the rules can be numbingly convoluted, taking into account income, marital status, whether you contribute to an employer-sponsored retirement savings plan, whether you file a joint or individual tax return, and whether both you and your spouse work or whether one or both of you are unemployed or self-employed. And then there's the question of whether you're talking about a tax-deductible IRA, a nondeductible IRA, a Roth IRA, or a SEP IRA for self-employed workers. And all of those variables can intertwine in different ways, resulting in varying degrees of eligibility.

Just to make the calculations really devious, how much you can contribute each year changes based on how those various factors interact. And if you're fifty or older, the calculations change a bit since, like the 401(k), you get to save a little more as part of the so-called catch-up provisions. Finally, the rules can be unforgiving in that many errors—especially the most common errors—cannot be corrected after the fact.

Because employers have nothing to do with an IRA, you'll have to open an IRA account at a brokerage firm, mutual fund, bank, or other purveyor of investment assets. Just go online and type "traditional IRA" into any search engine, and a number of providers will pop up. (If you don't include the word *traditional*, be prepared to surf through a wave of information on George and Ira Gerswhin, the International Reading Association, and the Irish Republican Army.)

Unlike a 401(k), IRA investment options are as numerous as ants in an ant hill. You're not limited to a relatively narrow selection of mutual funds or company stock. In an IRA you can invest in just about any traditional investment—stocks, bonds, mutual funds, annuities, options contracts, etc.—and several nontraditional assets such as real estate, promissory notes, and precious-metal coins, among others.

As with most tax-advantaged retirement savings accounts, if you tap your IRA before you're 59½, you'll pay taxes on the original contributions and the earnings, and a penalty equal to 10% of the value of the withdrawal. IRAs are taxed—at retirement or if withdrawn early—at ordinary income rates, which in 2005 are generally higher than capital gains rates.

Speaking of retirement: If you don't begin to draw on your IRA earlier in retirement, then at some point the government forces you to withdraw in what is known as a "required distribution." You must begin taking distributions from your account by April 1 of the year after the year in which you turn 70½ (so if you hit 70½ on November 8, 2005, you must begin to withdraw by April 1, 2006). Don't, and you face a steep penalty of 50% of the amount of money you should have withdrawn.

In the year that an account holder is supposed to begin taking distributions, IRA providers send a letter to the IRS announcing that fact. So the IRS knows that you should be drawing down your account. The good news is that the IRA provider sends the same letter to you. At the very least, then, you'll be notified well in advance so that you don't get hit with the penalty.

Tax-deductible IRA

Generally speaking, you can contribute in 2006 up to $4,000 in a tax-deductible IRA, meaning you can claim a deduction of as much as $4,000 on your income taxes for the year. In 2008 the annual contribution limit jumps to $5,000, and thereafter it is indexed to inflation. Baby boomers who hit fifty in a given year can save up to an additional $1,000 starting in 2006.

	Regular	Catch-up
2005	$ 4,000	$ 500
2006	4,000	1,000
2007	4,000	1,000
2008	5,000	1,000
2009+	Indexed*	1,000

*Normal contribution limits in 2009 and 2010 will be $5,000 plus an amount indexed to inflation.

The actual size of the deduction you're eligible for—and thus the size of the contribution you can make in a given year—depends on the factors mentioned above. Consider, for instance, this purposefully complex example in which you and a spouse both want to contribute to separate IRAs: You contribute to your company's retirement savings plan; your spouse doesn't work and so isn't eligible for a retirement plan; and your adjusted gross income (AGI) on a joint tax return for 2005 is $79,000. In that situation you can contribute only $200 to an IRA because your AGI falls within the $70,000 to $80,000 range in which eligibility begins to phase out. Your spouse can contribute the maximum amount to an IRA, however, because the family's AGI is well below the range in which a spousal contribution phases out.

Just because you are qualified to contribute a certain amount of money to a deductible IRA doesn't mean you must contribute that amount. You can contribute as much as you want up to the maximum amount for which you qualify; however, you can deduct from your taxes only what you contribute.

The deductibility of your contributions to an IRA depends on your tax-filing status, your income, and whether you, your spouse, or both of you participate in a company-sponsored retirement savings plan.

In written form the deductibility rules seem as clear as the technical explanations for programming a VCR. So below you'll find a graphical representation of IRS Publication 590, which details deductibility guidelines. This is for the 2004 tax year. The income limits will increase over time.

			Married, filing jointly			
			Spouse participates in employer's plan		Spouse doesn't participate in employer's plan	
Modified Adjusted Gross Income ($)	Single					
	You participate in employer's plan	You don't participate in employer's plan	You participate in employer's plan	You don't participate in employer's plan	You participate in employer's plan	You don't participate in employer's plan
Below 45,000	Full	Full	Full	Full	Full	Full
45,000 to 54,999	Partial	Full	Full	Full	Full	Full
55,000 to 64,999	None	Full	Full	Full	Full	Full
65,000 to 74,999	None	Full	Partial	Full	Partial	Full
75,000 to 150,000	None	Full	None	Full	None	Full
150,001 to 159,999	None	Full	None	Partial	None	Full
160,000 and above	None	Full	None	None	None	Full

NONDEDUCTIBLE IRA

As the name implies, contributions made to this type of IRA are not deductible on your taxes. So why would anyone contribute if they can't take the deduction? Well, the money still grows tax-deferred, and that's a benefit. Moreover, because you didn't take a tax deduction for your original contributions, you have the right to reclaim that money without paying taxes or a penalty.

But beware: You can't just decide to withdraw from your nontaxable IRA first and then draw down your taxable IRA later. The IRS requires that you withdraw the money proportionately. For instance, if you have $5,000 in a nondeductible IRA and $45,000 in a deductible IRA, and you withdraw $5,000 for some need, only 10% of the cash you take out is tax-free (5,000 ÷ 50,000 in total IRA accounts). You'll owe taxes on the other 90%.

In practice, nondeductible IRAs are best used as the IRA of last resort. If your income disqualifies you for other types of IRAs, then at the very least you can contribute to one of these. The only stipulation is that you must report earned income for the year. The size of your contribution is limited to your earned income or the annual IRA contribution maximum, whichever is smaller.

TAKE NOTE

Don't commingle your deductible and nondeductible IRA money. The paperwork will be easier on you if you keep the accounts separate.

Also, be aware that if you open a nondeductible IRA, you *must* file a bit of extra paperwork—IRS Form 8606—with your taxes. It tells the IRS that you have a nondeductible IRA. However, if you forget to file this form, then a few bad things happen, one worse than the others. The least painful: You owe a $50 penalty for failure to file the form, stretching back to when you first opened the account. So if you don't report your nondeductible IRA on Form 8606 for three years, well, then, you'll owe the government $150 plus interest. The IRS can also levy a $100 penalty for overstating the value of your nondeductible account, so it's not wise to tell the agency that all or most of your money was in a nondeductible IRA—unless, of course, that's actually true.

Worse: If you cannot show the IRS that you filed Form 8606, then when you go to withdraw your money years later in retirement, you'll owe taxes on your contributions even though those dollars should not be taxed.

THE ROTH

The Roth IRA, named for Delaware Senator William V. Roth, Jr., is the closest thing to a free lunch that anyone in government or on Wall Street will ever offer investors—and the strings that are attached aren't so bad.

Roth rules allow you to save after-tax dollars in an account that grows tax-free. Essentially, your contributions and the subsequent earnings grow without being taxed, and then when you withdraw the money in retirement, you get to bypass the tax man again. That's huge, making the Roth one of the most valuable retirement savings accounts.

It only gets better. Because you've already paid taxes on your contributions before you invested them in a Roth, you can withdraw the total amount of your annual contributions—at any time for any reason—without paying taxes or a penalty. That is nice if you stumble into financial straits and need access to money. You can also pull out the earnings tax-free—as long as you are at least 59½ and you've had the account at least five years. Just to sweeten the Roth a little more, you're not required to take distributions ever, meaning the account can pass to a beneficiary, who, in turn, will draw down the money tax-free—or pass what is left at their death to their beneficiary, ultimately creating a potentially vast store of family wealth over time.

The only substantial caveat is that the IRS doesn't allow you to take any income tax deductions for the money you save in a Roth. Also, not everyone is eligible to contribute because Roths limit your ability to contribute once you hit certain income levels. In 2006, Roth eligibility phases out for people who are single and report adjusted gross income of between $95,000 and $110,000. Below $95,000 you can contribute fully to a Roth; above $110,000 you can contribute nothing. Between those bookends you can make a partial contribution depending on where your income falls. The phaseout occurs between $150,000 and $160,000 on a joint return.

SEP IRAS AND KEOGH PLANS

These are specifically designed for self-employed workers who otherwise wouldn't have a company-sponsored retirement-savings plan.

Both have the same contribution limits: 20% of your net self-employed income (defined as your annual revenue minus deductions) or 25% of your wages, up to a maximum of $42,000 in 2005. The contribution limits ratchet up each year based on cost-of-living adjustments. To determine whether you can contribute 20% or 25%, take this quick test:

- If your annual earnings are reported on a W-2, you're a wage earner eligible to contribute up to 25% of those wages.

- If your annual earnings are reported on Schedule C or E, you have self-employment income and you're eligible to contribute up to 20% of your net self-employment income.

With a SEP IRA (Simplified Employee Pension IRA) your employer—basically your business—contributes the cash. If your business can't swing a contribution or you don't want your business to make one in a particular year, you don't have to. SEP plans must be funded by the April 15 tax-filing deadline plus any extensions you file.

Keogh plans, meanwhile, come in two different types: a money-purchase plan and a profit-sharing plan.

- Money-purchase plan: The contribution each year is mandatory whether you have profits or not.

- Profit-sharing plan: The contribution each year is discretionary, meaning if you have no net profits, you don't have to contribute

Keogh plans must be opened by December 31 of the year in which you claim the deduction, but you have until April 15, plus extensions, to fund it. Also, Keogh plans tend to have more paperwork associated with them.

BORROWING FROM YOUR IRA

You can't. Don't even try. Rules forbid it. IRA providers won't let you. IRA providers don't even have applications for you to fill out.

Of course, there is a loophole.

Once every twelve months IRA rules allow you to roll your account or some portion of it from one provider to another. In doing so the IRS gives you sixty days to get the cash into the new account. That means you have two months to do whatever you want with the money as long as you place into the new account the exact dollar amount, to the penny, that you withdrew from the original account. In essence, this is a short-term loan option built into an IRA if you ever need the cash.

This is a risky strategy, however. You might have every intention of replacing the cash you've "borrowed," but after spending on what prompted the loan in the first place, you might suddenly find that you can't replace the money. You will now have to come up with additional dollars to pay the taxes and penalty you'll owe on the withdrawal.

The best advice is don't risk it unless you are absolutely, positively certain that you will have the money in the new account before the IRS cares.

RAISING CASH IN RETIREMENT

People often get to a point in retirement where their income doesn't meet their financial needs. Maybe you've overspent in retirement; maybe you didn't have enough money saved to begin with. Whatever the reason, you realize one morning that your needs exceed your means, and you either must find a new source of income or cut back your living drastically.

There are two potential assets that retirees often overlook: a home and a life insurance policy. Both can provide a

DON'T DO IT: WRONG INVESTMENTS IN RIGHT ACCOUNTS

Various types of investments have various types of tax advantages. So, too, do the various types of investment accounts. Incorrectly mixing the two saps your returns, costing you money.

Take, for instance, municipal bonds (which are discussed in the Investing section). The income they generate is not taxed at any level. Thus, it makes no sense to keep them in a tax-deferred retirement account like an IRA or a 401(k); if you're not paying taxes to begin with, there's no benefit from tax deferral. As such, municipal bonds are best suited for traditional taxable accounts such as a brokerage account.

Here are a variety of investments and an explanation of where you should hold them to the degree that you can. These are general rules of thumb; specific tax situations should be discussed with your financial or accounting pro:

Investment	Taxable Account	Tax-deferred Account	Comment
Annuities	✔		Annuities are tax-deferred to begin with.
Corporate bonds		✔	Income is taxable at generally higher ordinary-income rates.
Growth stocks/ Small-cap stocks	✔	a	Long-term capital gains are 15%, lower than most ordinary-income rates. (a) If you expect your ordinary-income rate will be low in retirement, let profits from these fast growers accumulate in a tax-deferred account.
High-yield stocks	✔		Dividend tax rates are 15%, much lower than the ordinary-income rates you'd pay withdrawing the money from a tax-deferred account later.

Investment	Taxable Account	Tax-deferred Account	Comment
Master Limited Partnerships (MLPs)		✔	MLPs generally don't throw off dividends that qualify for the 15% tax rate. You want them to grow tax-deferred.
Municipal bonds	✔		Free from local, state, and federal taxes.
Preferred stock	a	b	Some preferred dividends are actually interest. (a) Those that pay true dividends go into taxable accounts. (b) Those that pay interest should be in tax-deferred accounts.
Real estate investment trusts (REITs)		✔	REITs generally avoid corporate taxes, passing that burden to shareholders. Their dividends generally don't qualify for the 15% rate. Let them grow tax-deferred.
Treasury bonds	✔		Free from local and state taxes

substantial income, and with the home, at least, you don't have to sell it to turn it into a pile of cash.

THE REVERSE MORTGAGE

This might appear to belong in the Borrowing section on home mortgages, but it is better suited to retirement planning because of what a reverse mortgage does: It allows retirees to tap the equity in their home for retirement expenses they might otherwise have a hard time covering or might have to ask their children to help them pay for. The best part is that you don't have to sell your home and move to a less expensive place. Nor do you have to take out a home-equity loan and then make monthly payments. Instead, the lender pays *you.*

A reverse mortgage works exactly like a traditional mortgage—only in reverse. A lender determines the value of your home and then either sends you monthly payments over several years, gives you a lump sum of cash, or provides a credit line that you draw on whenever you like without having the traditional monthly note to repay. If you want, you can combine any of those payment options, receiving a partial lump sum and then monthly payments. You can even select an option in which you receive a payment every month for as long as you live even if you live to be the oldest human alive.

The loan is repaid when you, your heirs, or your estate sell the house. Like a traditional mortgage, there is an interest rate involved. The interest accumulates each month and must be repaid on top of the cumulative payments the lender has given you. As such, a reverse mortgage is a "rising debt, falling equity" mortgage, meaning that with each payment you receive, your loan balance increases. That's the opposite of a traditional mortgage, in which your equity rises and your debt falls with each payment.

Here is a simple example of what the "rising debt, falling value" proposition looks like in the first five years of a reverse mortgage. This assumes you receive a $1,000 monthly payment from a lender charging 6% annually (or 0.5% per month) on a home with a current value of $250,000 that is rising in value at 3% a year.

Year	Cumulative Principal Advances	Accumulated interest	Loan Balance	Home Value	Home Equity
1	$12,000	$ 397	$12,397	$257,500	$245,103
2	24,000	1,559	25,559	265,225	239,666
3	36,000	3,533	39,533	273,182	233,649
4	48,000	6,368	54,368	281,377	227,009
5	60,000	10,119	70,119	289,819	219,700

To obtain a reverse mortgage you must own your home, and all the owners of the home generally must be at least sixty-two years old. Your home must be your principal residence, which means you must live there more than half the year, and it must be debt-free. To the last point, most people who take out a reverse mortgage while still paying down a traditional mortgage use an immediate cash advance to pay off their traditional mortgage and then take smaller monthly payments to spend as they wish—on travel, health care costs, daily living expenses, the price of a long-term care insurance policy, or whatever.

The amount of money available in a reverse mortgage depends on your age, the value of your home, and prevailing interest rates. The older you are, the more money you'll receive since the value of the loan you're eligible for is spread over a shorter life expectancy.

When the house is sold, the outstanding balance is repaid and any remaining money goes to you, your estate, or your heirs. Under no circumstances, however, will you or your heirs have to repay more than the value of the house even if the monthly payments you received over the years greatly exceed that value. Reverse mortgages are nonrecourse loans, meaning a lender cannot go after your income or your heirs' income in the event the repayment falls short of the outstanding balance. In that situation the lender has made a bad bet and must eat the loss.

Just remember that you are consuming your equity with a reverse mortgage. As a result you will leave a smaller estate to your heirs, and if they don't have other funds to draw on, they could be forced to sell the family home to repay the loan after your death.

The most comprehensive, unbiased data on reverse mortgages is found online at the AARP Web site (www.aarp.org) and at www.reverse.org, a provider of no-nonsense consumer-oriented information on reverse-mortgage pros and cons.

LIFE SETTLEMENTS:
SELLING YOUR LIFE INSURANCE POLICY

Like a reverse mortgage, this probably seems better suited for another section of this guide, perhaps the one on Insurance. But, again, this is a financial product geared toward seniors wanting to raise cash for various expenses in retirement.

In essence, if you have active life insurance policies you no longer need or on which you no longer want to pay the premiums, you can sell them to investors for cash. This even goes for term life policies, which policy owners frequently allow to lapse when they no longer need the coverage, assuming that since term life has no built-up cash value, it's worthless unless you die. You do not have to be chronically ill or dying to sell your policy, though you do generally need to be at least sixty-five years old and the face value of your policy, or the combined value of multiple policies, generally must be $250,000 or more.

Investors buy the policies and continue to pay the premiums for as long as you live, and then when you die, they are the beneficiaries who receive the life insurance payout. That means your beneficiary gets nothing. For that reason reputable life-settlement companies—and there are those that aren't—routinely require that beneficiaries agree to the sale up front.

How much money you'll receive for your policy depends on factors ranging from your age, the value of the policy, the type of policy, your life expectancy, your health, and the size of your premium payments. In general, owners of universal policies, which combine a death benefit with a savings component, typically receive at least three times the underlying cash value of the policy. With term life policies, the kind that you pay premiums for a set number of years and then the policy goes away, younger, healthier retirees might get 10% to 15% of the policy's face value, while older, ailing retirees could get 30% or more.

RETIREMENT WITHDRAWALS

Though it sounds like a retiree longing to return to a career, *retirement withdrawals* refers to the amount of money you can safely pull from your nest egg every year without running out of money over time.

Research has shown that a withdrawal rate of about 4.1% of your portfolio should allow your money to last at least as long as you do. This represents the *initial* withdrawal rate, meaning the first year's withdrawal only. In subsequent years your withdrawal should increase to match the rate of inflation.

For instance, if you start with a $1 million portfolio, you would withdraw $41,000 in year one. If inflation is running at, say, 2.5%, then in year two you withdraw $42,205 (41,000 × 1.025). Assuming inflation stays constant, by year five you would be withdrawing $45,256.

If you withdraw too aggressively—and anything much beyond about 5% begins to get aggressive—you risk running out of money too soon. That's because investment returns ebb and flow annually, and if you're withdrawing at your normal, aggressive rate in a down year, your portfolio isn't likely to be able to replenish that. With a smaller withdrawal rate, your portfolio can survive longer. You can tell yourself you'll just take out less after a down year, but few people actually do that. Who wants to take a dramatic income cut when a less aggressive initial withdrawal rate means you don't have to?

❧

But there are risks to consider. If you need insurance for any reason, such as providing for a spouse after your death or to leave an estate to your heirs, then selling your policy is a mistake because obtaining new insurance at an advanced age may be impossible or prohibitively expensive. Also, while life insurance payouts to your beneficiary are tax-free, the proceeds from the sale of an insurance contract are not. So you'll owe taxes on the income.

COLLEGE PLANNING

In 2005 the average public university cost nearly $11,400 a year for tuition, fees, room, and board. Private schools averaged more than $27,500. Over four years that is enough to pay for a spiffy sports car or, in some cities, a respectable house.

But like so many financial obligations, averages don't say a whole lot about the specific schools you or your children might be interested in attending. The Internet is chockablock with college cost calculators, and some are better than others. One of the better ones is found under the Investment Planning & Tools tab at www.troweprice.com, the Web address of investment and mutual fund firm T. Rowe Price. The calculator allows you to gauge the projected costs at any of hundreds of specific colleges and junior colleges around the country. That gives you a better sense of your true target. After all, if you're aiming for the average cost of a state school education, you're in for a shock if your child has in mind the University of Michigan, where the all-in cost for the 2005–2006 academic year was more than $18,600 for an incoming freshman. ✎ *page 88*

College Savings Accounts

Essentially three main educational savings options exist: Coverdell Education Savings Accounts (formerly Education IRAs), a 529 college savings plan, and custodial accounts such as UGMA and UTMA, both of which hold irrevocable financial gifts to minors.

Each account has its pros and cons.

Coverdell accounts: These are designed much like an IRA in that they allow you to save money tax-deferred. If you withdraw the cash for "qualified" educational expenses, the earnings are tax-free. If you take the money for any other reason, you pay taxes on the gains at ordinary income rates as well as a 10%

penalty. As with an IRA, you can invest in an endless variety of mutual funds. Unlike an IRA, however, you cannot deduct the annual contributions on your tax returns. Coverdells are unique in that the money saved in these accounts can also be used to pay for private school costs before college.

If your child decides one day to join a touring mime troupe instead of attending college, you can change a Coverdell's beneficiary as long as all of the following are true:

- The trust agreement (the paperwork you received when opening the account) allows for beneficiary changes.

- The existing beneficiary is under the age of thirty.

- The new beneficiary is under the age of thirty.

- The new beneficiary is a member of the existing beneficiary's family.

Coverdells do have several Achilles' heels: First, federal law allows you to save only $2,000 per year per child. That means if you contribute $1,500 in a given year, then a grand-parent, another relative, or a family friend can contribute only $500. While the growth of $2,000 could be a respectable sum over time, with college costs escalating at about 8% a year historically, that relatively small savings rate makes it tough to save a sizable amount for college if that's your goal. Moreover, your ability to contribute begins to phase out for single wage earners who in 2005 made $95,000 to $110,000 and for joint tax filers who earned between $190,000 and $220,000 combined. (Those phaseout limits ratchet up occasionally, so it's best to check with the IRS, which publishes the information in Form 5305-EA, which you can find online by searching the IRS Web site at www.irs.gov.)

Finally, Coverdell accounts must be distributed by the time

the beneficiary reaches age thirty; otherwise the balance is forcibly distributed, with the earnings taxed as ordinary income and penalized an additional 10%.

529 plans: These plans are operated by states or educational institutions, and every state has at least one; some have more. Much like Coverdells, 529 plans, named for a section of the IRS tax code, allow you to save tax-deferred. Again, if you withdraw the money to pay for qualified educational expenses, the earnings are tax-free. Use the money for noneducational expenses, and it's taxed just as Coverdells are. Some states offer additional tax advantages. The Web site www.savingforcollege. com offers the broadest data on each state's 529 plans as well as an evaluation tool to help you determine which states offer the best plans.

You don't have to invest in your state's plan; you can invest in any plan, and it pays to shop around since some plans are substantially better than others. Know, though, that investing in another state's plan may alter any state tax advantages you might be eligible for in your home state's plan. One key advantage parents universally like is that with a 529 plan you don't relinquish control of the assets, meaning that unlike custodial accounts, in particular, a beneficiary has no right to claim the money at a certain age.

529 Plans come in two flavors: prepaid and savings.

In a **prepaid plan,** you literally prepay the expenses for a set number of years of college courses or a preestablished number of college credits. In essence you lock in tomorrow's college costs today, since prepaid plans are guaranteed to rise alongside college tuition inflation. Thus, if you purchase a full year's tuition today, then your child will have a full year's tuition ready to go at an in-state public university even if college is still fifteen years away. If your child opts to go out of state or attend a private school, the plan typically pays the average in-state tuition and fees for schools in that particular state. Parents or the student will be responsible for costs that exceed that amount. Savingforcollege.com has links to all the states' prepaid plans.

Savings plans operate much like a Coverdell in that you save money periodically in mutual funds. Yet these have a big benefit over Coverdells because you can generally save about $250,000 per beneficiary, either over time or in one lump-sum payment. Moreover, the money doesn't have to be distributed by any particular age and you can roll the assets from one generation to the next. You can even name yourself the beneficiary if your kids or grandkids don't use the money and you decide to go back to school later in life. Unlike prepaid plans, however, you are not guaranteed to match college cost inflation. Depending on how your investments perform, you could outpace the rise in college tuition over the years—or fall far short.

Investment choices in 529 savings plans are usually limited to a small selection of mutual funds, often those that are pre-mixed for a particular risk tolerance. Parents of an infant might save in an aggressive account, while those with a high school sophomore would want something more secure so that an unexpected hiccup in the stock market wouldn't annihilate the accumulated value right before college. Many plans offer funds that moderate the risk over time, starting off aggressively and growing increasingly risk averse as the child ages.

The two types of 529 plans differ dramatically when it comes to financial aid. Prepaid plans have a big impact on aid eligibility, while the impact of a savings plan is more modest. Prepaid plans are deemed a "resource" by college aid administrators and reduce need-based financial aid by 100% of the value of the plan. Savings plans are seen as an "asset" of the parent, and federal financial aid formulas assume that a maximum of 5.64% of parents' assets are eligible to pay for higher education costs. More on this below in the sidebar "Demystifying the Federal Financial Aid Formula."

UGMA and UTMA: The initials stand for Uniform Gifts to Minors Act and Uniform Transfers to Minors Act. They are essentially the same thing: an irrevocable gift of cash or securities made to a minor and managed by a custodian, which can be you or a financial professional you designate. These are the most flexible accounts because you can save as much money as you like and can invest across the broad spectrum of stocks, bonds, options, CDs, mutual funds, and more. UGMA and UTMA accounts are typically held at brokerage firms, mutual fund companies, banks, and trust companies.

Custodial accounts seem appealing in some instances. If the account generates substantial profits each year, much of it is taxed at the child's lower income tax rate, saving you money on your tax bill through the years. The accounts have other drawbacks, however, that often outweigh the tax savings.

The drawbacks include the fact that the earnings are taxed along the way even though it is at the child's income tax rate. Even a small amount of taxes is worse than paying no taxes, as on Coverdell and 529 accounts. Moreover, when it comes to financial aid calculations, half the value of these accounts is considered eligible to pay for college, substantially more than parents are generally on the hook for if the money were held in their name instead. Finally, parents lose control of the money, and once a child hits the "age of majority" (typically eighteen or twenty-one, depending on the state), the account must be distributed to the beneficiary—the child. That means your daughter, without your permission, can rush out to buy a candy-apple-red Corvette if she'd rather have that than finish her pre-med degree.

FINANCIAL AID

Financial aid comes from three sources: grants and scholarships, loans, and the Federal Work-Study program.

WHAT EXACTLY IS A QUALIFIED EDUCATION EXPENSE?

IRS Publication 970, which you can find at the IRS Web site, www.irs.gov, outlines what falls under the rubric of "qualified education expense." The list is short:

- Tuition and fees necessary to enroll in school.

- Expenses for special-needs services incurred by special-needs students.

- Books, supplies, and equipment necessary to participate in classes. Though the IRS publication doesn't spell this out, in some cases "equipment" can mean a laptop computer, for instance, if the school or a particular degree requires that students be able to access the school's Internet site for various educational reasons.

- Room and board.

Any other expenses are not covered.

❧

Grants and scholarships: This is free money since you don't have to repay it. These are awarded by governments, universities, charities, corporations, associations, foundations, fraternal orders, and private individuals, among others. Most scholarships are based on merit, not on a family's financial need. As such, a child typically must demonstrate some sort of academic, artistic, or athletic ability or some level of civic leadership. That's not always the case, though. The Henkel Corporation in Avon, Ohio, annually awards $5,000 in scholarship money to the high school couple that designs and wears the most creative prom attire fashioned entirely from the company's Duck-brand duct tape. Web sites such as www.fastweb.

com and www.collegeanswer.com provide comprehensive lists of millions of scholarships worth billions of dollars annually.

If your child has a strong desire to be, say, a chemist, economist, or nurse, check with that department at the university your child plans to attend. The various academic departments at numerous schools distribute their own scholarships to students pursuing a particular degree.

High school juniors and seniors should visit their guidance counselor's office often because counselors receive hundreds of local scholarship notices that university financial aid administrators often don't keep track of. These are generally small scholarships in the $500 to $1,000 range, though some are substantially larger. Apply for as many as you're eligible for. Keep your application material, such as any essays you're required to write; you can recycle that material with modest changes to ease the paperwork burden of seeking multiple scholarships.

One of the largest grant programs is the federal government's Pell Grants, which in 2004 doled out $12.7 billion, or about $2,466 per recipient. These grants are based solely on financial need as determined by the Free Application for Federal Student Aid, known as the Fafsa form. It is available online at fafsa.ed.gov. Colleges use the Fafsa form to determine eligibility for federal, state, and university scholarship and grant aid. Submit the Fafsa form to your child's college of choice as early in the year as possible; schools begin dispensing aid dollars for the coming academic year early in the spring.

Loans: If you don't accumulate enough dollars to pay for college through scholarships and grants, you can borrow. The federal Stafford Loan program is the largest; it dispensed nearly $50 billion in the 2003–2004 academic year. Two types of Stafford Loans are available:

- Subsidized: The federal government pays the interest while the student is in school, for the first six months after gradu-

DEMYSTIFYING THE FEDERAL FINANCIAL AID FORMULA

At its core the federal formula for determining how much aid a student is eligible for is based on the notion that parents and students bear some responsibility to whatever extent they're able to pay. That extent is called your EFC, or Expected Family Contribution.

The EFC formula takes into account the assets and income of parents and the student. The formula regards the following as available to pay college costs:

- 35% of a student's assets

- 50% of a student's income

- 2.6% to 5.6% of parents' assets

- 22% to 47% of parents' income

The formula takes into account the oldest parent's age, sheltering an increasingly larger amount of assets from the calculation the older a parent is, and it recognizes that parents have other costly expenses to save for, namely retirement. As such, assets in retirement plans are excluded from the formula. So, too, is the value of a primary residence.

In essence, assets earmarked for college are typically best held in the name of the parents unless Mom and Dad have a vast amount of assets held outside of retirement accounts. In that case, 5.6% of their assets may well exceed 50% of the child's assets.

This is another reason that it pays to save for retirement before college: You're maximizing not just your retirement savings but your child's chances of acquiring as much financial aid as possible.

ation, and, if necessary, for a period of deferment. Subsidized loans are awarded based solely on financial need as determined by the Fafsa form. The interest rate charged is variable.

- Unsubsidized: This is available to any student regardless of financial need. Students are responsible for interest payments from the outset, though while pursuing a degree a student can allow the interest to accrue and roll into the principal. The interest rate is also variable.

How much money a student is eligible for from a Stafford Loan depends on what academic year a student is in, whether the student is considered dependent on parents or is independent, and whether the student is in undergraduate or graduate school. For a breakdown of how much a student is eligible for, visit the federal student aid Web site at www. studentaid.ed.gov.

Parents also have a federal loan option to help pay a child's college costs—the Parent Loans for Undergraduate Students, or PLUS loans. Parents can borrow up to the total cost of college, minus whatever aid the student receives. There are no asset or income limits, though you must pass a credit check that shows you're not more than ninety days past due on any other debt obligations.

Information on all the federal loan and grant programs is available online at www.studentaid.ed.gov.

Private lenders are also big players in the college-loan market, led by SLM Corporation's Sallie Mae, Wells Fargo, Wachovia, and Bank of America. Smaller local banks also make education loans. With private lenders, though, be prepared to pay higher interest rates.

Work-Study: This is a federally funded, needs-based program in which students work part-time while they're in school to pay for the costs of a degree. Jobs are typically on campus, though in some situations the jobs can be off campus, often with a local community service program or public agency. The pay rate in 2005 ranged from minimum wage to $10 or $12 an hour, depending on the skills necessary for the job. Earnings cannot exceed the financial need determined by the Fafsa form.

CHAPTER 6

INSURANCE

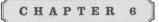

Insurance gets no respect.

While just about every other aspect of personal finance centers on accumulating wealth, insurance is all about spending money for a product that, if you need it, you know you've had a bad day. You've either been robbed, you've wrecked your car, your house has been damaged in a disaster, you've seriously injured yourself, you have an illness that has flared up, or, in the worst of all possible bad days, you have died.

For that reason people typically hate shelling out for an insurance policy, often grumbling about spending money year in and year out for something they rarely, maybe even never, use.

That's understandable. But how often do you call on the police department because of an emergency? How often do you call on the fire department to save your burning home? You may not need either for decades, but when you do, you're relieved they're around for the bad moments of your life.

Insurance is exactly the same. Without it, all the personal wealth you manage to amass is at risk when bad things happen to you or your property or to others injured by you or your property. In those situations all the money you've paid to own insurance through the years—the premiums—pays off, allowing you to replace your property, pay for expensive medical care, or cover the damages you inflicted on someone else.

All insurance is fairly similar in the way it works. When you buy an insurance policy, the insurer groups you with people similar to you in age, health status, sex, lifestyle, home location, and a variety of other factors. Then actuaries—vital statisticians who compute risk—calculate how many deaths, car accidents, heart transplants, hurricanes, or whatever are likely to occur over a period of time to your particular group of people. Insurers use that risk assessment to determine the premiums you must pay to insure whatever risk it is you're trying to mitigate—be it your premature death or the risk that an uninsured motorist will total your classic Corvette. With life insurance, for instance, if you're young and healthy, your premiums are low because statistically the chances are low that you will die soon and force the insurer to pay a benefit. On the other hand, if you're old and ailing, your premiums will be very high because the risk that you will die soon is substantially greater.

This pool of similar consumers essentially shares the risk of protecting one another from financial hardship in the event of death or some other insured event. This shared risk works because of the law of large numbers, a scientific principle in which the actions of one will not have a tremendous effect on the group as a whole at any given moment. Thus, a relatively small number of events each year that require an insurer to pay claims will not sharply impair the overall pool.

Insurance companies don't just sit on the premiums you pay; they invest them. Since statistically you're not likely to claim the money for years, if ever, the insurer can generate a return on those dollars to grow the asset base. Because of the investment return and because only a small portion of the insured population will file a claim in any given year, insurers have the ability to pay your claim for, say, $40,000 even though you might have paid the insurance company only $7,000 in premiums through the years.

Let's take a look at a typical insurance contract from the point of view of you, the average insurance buyer. The three key figures are coverage, premium, and deductible.

Coverage is how much money the policy will pay out for whatever event you are insuring, whether it's your life or the cost of rebuilding a beachfront home after a hurricane blows through. With life insurance, for instance, the coverage might be $100,000, meaning that when you die your beneficiary will receive a check for that amount.

Premium represents the cost of the coverage or how much you have to pay to buy the insurance policy. Though the coverage might be $100,000, your premium will be just a sliver of that because of the way insurance companies spread across millions of customers the risk you represent individually.

Insurance companies place people in one of four risk groups: preferred, standard, substandard, and uninsurable. Preferred customers are charged the lowest premiums; the uninsurable are, well, uninsurable for whatever reason. But remember this: A customer that one insurer labels preferred might be labeled standard by another, and at commensurately higher rates. Insurers routinely tighten and loosen their underwriting standards—the standards they use to determine who falls into what category—depending on a variety of business factors. Those standards can and do change regularly. The message is to shop around to find a cheaper premium for the same coverage.

> **RULE TO REMEMBER:**
>
> The higher the deductible, the lower your premium. So go with the highest deductible you can afford, and you'll save money in the long run. Just be sure to set aside some of the savings to cover the higher deductible you'll have to pay in the event you ever file a claim.

Deductible is how much money you have to come up with to help cover the cost of an insurable event. If you have a $250 deductible on your auto insurance and you wreck your classic Gremlin, causing $1,000 in damages to the car, you're responsible for the first $250; the insurance company covers the rest.

Many consumers often want the lowest deductible because they loathe the notion of digging up a big chunk of money in the event something happens that causes them to file a claim. It is better, they feel, to pay as small an amount as possible and let the insurer do the heavy lifting. That is a more expensive proposition in the long run. Here's why: If you double a $500 deductible to $1,000, you might save $150 a year on your premiums. Sure, you're on the hook now for an extra $500, but you'll come out ahead financially because every 3.3 years you will have saved $500 in premiums ($500 ÷ 150 = 3.3$) you'd otherwise have to pay with a lower deductible. That makes it a pretty simple equation: If you're not filing claims very often, why pay the higher premiums for no reason? And if you are filing claims often, then it's a moot point: Your insurance company is going to jack up your premiums anyway or cancel your coverage because you obviously present a greater risk to the company.

Now let's take a look at the types of insurance most consumers deal with.

LIFE INSURANCE

Despite the name, life insurance isn't so much about life as it is about death. In fact, if you insure your life, you'll never benefit from the money since the insurance company pays the so-called death benefit—the face value of the policy—to the policy's beneficiary only after the sand has run out of your hourglass.

With certain types of policies you can accumulate cash through the years that you can draw on later in life while you're still breathing—what is known as a *cash-value* policy. These are akin to a savings account wrapped in an insurance contract. We'll get to these in a minute.

Essentially, life insurance is available in two basic forms: term life and cash value—and there is a never-ending "tastes great, less filling" feud that surrounds these two options. Proponents of term insurance argue that it is cheaper, more cost-effective coverage. The cash-value crowd insists their policies, also known as permanent insurance, offer an investment component that helps you build wealth. In truth, both types of coverage have their pros and cons.

Term life insurance, as the name suggests, is in place for a specific number of years—the term. That term is typically between ten and thirty years, though different terms are available. You determine how much insurance coverage you need—say $100,000—and you pay a premium, usually monthly, that guarantees your beneficiary will be paid the face value of the policy (that $100,000) if you die during the term in which your policy is in place. With some policies the premiums rise each year, starting off small and growing increasingly more expensive. With a **level term** policy your premiums never change, though they will be somewhere between the low and high end of a policy where the premium increases annually.

The biggest benefit of term insurance is that it is the cheapest type of life insurance, meaning you can afford more coverage for a relatively small premium. As a nonsmoking, healthy thirty-year-old, you might pay about $125 a year for twenty years of $100,000 coverage.

The biggest pitfall is that if you're still alive at the end of the term, the policy goes away and you have nothing to show for all those years of premiums you paid.

In many instances term policies come with annual renewal provisions that allow you to continue coverage each year after the original term has ended. Eligibility for the continuing coverage may be automatic, meaning that you don't have to requalify medically; in other cases you might have to requalify with a medical exam. In either case your premiums will be higher, possibly substantially, since you're now years older and possibly in worse health. Guaranteed renewability—a guarantee that the policy cannot be canceled because of poor health if you decide to renew your coverage when the original policy terminates—is standard on most good policies. You should not buy any insurance policy that does not have this feature.

Also, while a term policy does not build cash along the way, some can be converted into a cash-value policy at some point, if you desire, without a physical exam. If you think you'll ever want a cash-value policy, make sure your term policy offers this option.

Cash-value insurance is life insurance with a built-in savings element that accumulates over time. Part of the premium you pay each month buys a death benefit, while the other portion goes into the cash account. Because of this dual structure, cash-value policy premiums are typically four to eight times that of a similarly sized term insurance policy. For instance, that $100,000 term life coverage that cost $125 might cost $1,000 a year as a cash-value policy.

Cash-value insurance comes in a variety of styles, such as whole life, variable life, universal life, and variable universal life. Depending on what you buy, the cash account earns dividends that grow at a fixed rate or are put to work in investments that you choose and that grow at a variable rate. The advantage of saving this way is that the money grows tax-deferred, meaning you pay no taxes on the cash value until you withdraw the money. At that point the government taxes the accumulated profits at higher, ordinary income rates.

You can employ the cash buildup in several ways: surrender the policy and claim the cash value; use the cash value to pay the premiums at some point; or borrow against the policy. If you borrow and happen to die with the loan outstanding, the insurer will deduct from the beneficiary's payout the remaining loan amount plus interest.

Cash-value premiums generally remain the same over the period in which you own the insurance. However, unlike term insurance, the policy doesn't go away after a set period of time. As long as you continue to pay the premiums, the policy remains in effect. The most important point to remember about cash-value policies is that they're designed to be held for life. Because your premiums must first cover substantial costs such as the sales commission, most contracts don't break even for fourteen or fifteen years, meaning that the premiums you've paid finally equal the accumulated cash value you're eligible to claim after that many years. Let the policy lapse—and the majority of policies do lapse—and you can lose lots of money.

If you're dead set on a cash-value policy, however, consider a no-load cash-value policy that imposes no commissions or surrender fees. You break even after the first year. Many insurers offer these for large enough policies, and some, such as USAA (www.usaa.com), offer them for much smaller policies that average consumers can buy.

Return-of-premium insurance is a relatively new entrant and is designed to bridge the chasm between term life and cash value. Basically, return-of-premium offers the benefits of term insurance but with a bonus: Outlive the policy, and the insurance company will return all the premiums you paid through the years.

In truth, when the financial services industry attempts to fashion a hybrid product meant to appeal to everyone, it basically creates what Dr. Seuss fans might know as a tizzle-topped Tufted Mazurka from the African island of Yerka—a peculiar creature you're probably better off without.

In short, return-of-premium policies are not so great. You pay a premium higher than you do with a traditional term policy, with that extra bit of money earning a bit of interest so that if you don't die and ultimately reclaim the funds, they will have grown—somewhat. The return, however, is generally smaller than you'd pocket by simply investing that extra bit of money in a certificate of deposit.

WHY BUY LIFE INSURANCE?

The most important asset you own is your ability to earn an income. Since you don't know if you're going to die tomorrow or fifty years from now, or somewhere in between, life insurance erases the uncertainties, providing a source of income to your family in the event you or your spouse dies prematurely. The insurer typically pays out a lump sum that a wise beneficiary invests and draws on over time to help cover various costs.

In some instances life insurance can serve as an estate-planning tool, but that's generally for people with large multi-million-dollar estates. So we'll keep this discussion to the basics of using life insurance to replace a lost income.

But Do I Need Life Insurance?

That depends on who you are. Let's start with the folks who generally *don't* need life insurance, which includes the following:

- Single people with no dependents to provide for.

- Working couples without kids and for which the premature death of one partner would not impact the ability of the survivor to pay the daily costs of life—although a small policy can help pay funeral costs because the price tag on dying these days is upwards of $10,000.

- Retirees who no longer have financial obligations such as a mortgage or the college expenses of a child to worry about.

- Wealthy people who already have an estate large enough to provide for a spouse's lifestyle.

- Children—though this comes with a caveat. Unless you live off the earnings of a child actor, kids are not sources of income, so there's generally little reason to insure their lives. However, buying insurance on a child can provide one benefit: It ensures the child's insurability later in life. If a child develops an illness such as diabetes, finding insurance will be a bear. If you have insurance in place prior to the onset of an illness, the policy remains in force and can often be extended, though the cost will increase.

You need life insurance under these conditions:

- You have dependent children. The loss of your income could affect your spouse's ability to remain in the family home with the kids or provide the level of education you otherwise could afford on your salary.

- You're married to a nonworking spouse. Your death will likely impact your spouse's ability to provide for the costs of life since going to work for the first time or after a long hiatus could mean a lower-paying job and a much diminished standard of living.

- You have a working spouse whose income is substantially less than yours. For many of the same reasons as above you should consider life insurance because your higher income affords a lifestyle your spouse couldn't afford alone.

- You have special-needs siblings or others you support or wish to care for.

- You still have a large mortgage remaining on your home. A life insurance payout will help a spouse pay off or pay down the balance, easing the financial burden after your death. But beware: In the weeks and months after you obtain a mortgage you will inevitably be bombarded by offers of "mortgage insurance," a policy that provides the funds necessary to pay off the mortgage on the family home if you or your spouse dies. Don't bite. These are essentially term life policies but are usually priced higher. Instead, if you want funds to repay the mortgage, factor that into your needs with a standard policy.

SHOULD I INSURE A STAY-AT-HOME SPOUSE?

Yes, particularly if that stay-at-home spouse takes care of the family's kids. In this particular case the spouse is not a source of income that needs to be replaced but provides services that must be replaced, particularly child care during the day or after school while the other spouse works.

At a minimum, a relatively small policy on a nonworking spouse will provide the income needed to pay for services that the working spouse otherwise would have to do or pay someone else to do.

How Much Life Insurance Is Enough?

The ideal amount of life insurance allows beneficiaries and dependents to invest the insurance payout and then draw down the account over time to maintain the standard of living that the missing income otherwise would have provided.

However, insurance isn't a one-size-fits-all financial product. Each family has different needs and different amounts of assets. It is probably obvious that the greater your financial need, the more insurance coverage you demand. But depending on the assets you have in place, the amount of insurance you need might be less.

You can use one of three methods—ranging from rudimentary to detailed—to calculate the appropriate level of coverage:

The Rule of Thumb is the most basic method, estimating that you need life insurance somewhere between five and ten times your annual salary. Those who use this method will often just split the difference and multiply their income by seven and call that enough coverage. If you bring in $50,000 a year, you'd need $350,000 of life insurance using this rule of thumb. Remember, though, to tally only the take-home pay, what you earn after taxes, since that is the true level of income you live on. There is no need to replace pre-tax income since a life insurance payout is not taxed.

This method is fairly simplistic in that it doesn't require you to address any specific insurance needs you might have, such as the cost of a child's college years from now or the continuing care of a special-needs dependent. Whatever your case, $350,000 may not be enough or may be too much. But if you don't want to go through the effort of figuring out exactly what you need, then the rule of thumb is better than nothing.

Income Replacement takes the view that you need to essentially replace some level of income—be it an entire salary or some portion of it—over a certain number of years. If you earn that same $50,000 but need to insure the replacement of all that income for at least seventeen years, you'd need an $850,000 policy—well beyond the top end of the rule-of-thumb method.

If you have few financial assets and no special needs to finance, then this method is likely a fine approach to use.

Financial Need takes into account various expenses your income would otherwise help afford, such as:

- A child's tuition

- The family's annual living expenses

- An emergency fund

- Your spouse's future retirement needs

- Debt/mortgage payoff

- Other special needs

This is the most detailed approach to life insurance because it requires some real thought to determine what expenses you need to cover and how much those expenses are going to cost years or decades from now. But it can be done relatively easily. With tuition, for instance, you can check out the college cost calculator at the T. Rowe Price Web site (www.troweprice.com) for an idea on expected tuition and other university fees at specific colleges any number of years from today. That will help you plan for the appropriate coverage.

With this method you should also evaluate the liquid assets you already have in place. If you have already saved for much of your child's expected college costs, there's really little reason to include that in your insurance coverage. ✎ *page 58*

Where to Invest an Insurance Payout

The first few years' worth of expenses should be invested in low-risk, guaranteed-return investments such as certificates of deposit, Treasury notes, and a savings account. This is money that you know you must depend on to pay living expenses, and you want to know the money is not subject to losses.

What defines "the first few years" is fairly subjective and depends largely on how many years the payout is intended to last. A payout anticipated to cover just five years should probably be entirely in guaranteed-return investments, since during any given five-year stretch you can't be sure if the stock or bond market will go up, down, or sideways.

If the money is to last twenty years, then put the first five years' worth in the guaranteed accounts and put the remaining payout in a mix of stock and bond mutual funds. Over such a long stretch you can rest assured that the stock market will go up and will grow faster than inflation, while the bond funds will provide necessary stability and income.

BUY TERM AND INVEST THE DIFFERENCE

Here's a rule to remember: Life insurance is not an investment—despite all the insistences to the contrary you're likely to hear from insurance agents and others. Do you buy a savings account with your auto insurance? How about a savings account to go along with your home owner's policy? Of course not.

You buy insurance for one reason: to *insure*, to protect against what would be a potentially catastrophic financial loss for you or your family. That is generally the only reason to own insurance. An insurance policy is not a savings or investment account, although agents will offer arguments that sound very convincing, such as the following:

"Insurance will be too expensive to buy when you're older." That's

true. Life insurance premiums rise dramatically as you grow older and closer to death. What that argument misses, though, is the fact that when you're older, you often don't need life insurance to begin with since you have no employment income to protect, no kids to send to school, and often no mortgage to worry about (or if you do have a mortgage, it's probably so small that it's not a burden).

"Whole life/universal life forces you to save money." True again. But, again, that's just half the argument. Saving through an insurance contract is an expensive way to save, and the returns are generally mediocre at best. If you must be forced into saving, then invest in your company's retirement savings plan since that money is pulled from your paycheck before you touch it and before it's taxed, a big benefit to you. Or use the money that otherwise would go into the higher whole-life premiums and invest it in an IRA. You can set up an IRA so that a certain amount of money is automatically withdrawn from your checking or savings account every month or quarter, forcing you to save painlessly. With the IRA you may also be eligible for a tax deduction. Buying a whole-life insurance policy affords you no tax deduction.

If you're already saving in a 401(k) plan or IRA, then ask your payroll department to draw money from your paycheck and place it in a credit union account or some other bank account. Or ask your bank to systematically take money from your checking account weekly or monthly and put it into a money-market account. Whatever the approach, there are much savvier ways to forcibly save than through an expensive whole-life insurance contract.

"Savings in a whole-life policy grow tax-deferred." True as well. But when you claim the money, the profits are taxed at ordinary income rates that can be substantially higher than capital gains rates applied to other investment accounts. If you are already saving in a company-sponsored retirement savings plan or an IRA, those tend to be much better tax-deferred accounts

because they offer better investment options and, at least with the company plan, usually a company match. Moreover, you don't want too much of your savings stuck inside tax-deferred accounts. If you ever need your money early and all you have are tax-deferred accounts to tap, your profits will be pecked away by a bigger tax bite and a penalty.

"Whole-life policies are all paid up after so many years, meaning you won't have to pay for your insurance anymore." True. But that's financial subterfuge. Here is the rest of the story: At some point the cash value in your account will reach a level at which the insurer can simply draw down the cash to pay the premiums. But that's your money anyway, so no matter how you look at it, you're still paying for the coverage. In essence, you've simply prepaid for coverage in later years by dumping so much money into the policy in the early years. It's not as if the insurance company is giving you something for free. Moreover, if the rate of return inside the cash-value component doesn't live up to the insurance company's projections, then at some point when your cash value can no longer cover the premiums, you will be asked to pony up more dollars to continue your coverage—or your coverage will go away.

Generally, the best approach to life insurance is to buy term insurance and invest the difference. If $100,000 of term life coverage costs $125 a year and the same amount of whole-life coverage costs $1,000, your finances will be much stronger if you buy the term policy and then stuff the savings of $875 a year into an investment account. To make it as painless as possible, ask a mutual fund company to automatically pull from your checking account $73 a month, the monthly equivalent of $875 a year. You'll never miss the money (after all, you were willing to spend it on whole-life premiums); you're forcing yourself to save just as you would inside the whole-life policy; and your returns are likely to be substantially superior since you're not paying the often pricey fees embedded in a cash-value policy.

ANNUITIES

Annuities could just as easily fit in the chapter on Investing because annuities are most often purchased as an investment. Nevertheless, they are a form of insurance—so here they are in the Insurance chapter.

At its most basic, an annuity is an insurance contract in which an insurer promises to pay the annuitant—that's you—a set amount of money periodically, generally monthly, for some span of years. That span can be for just a few years or stretch for as long as you continue to live. Used appropriately, an annuity can be an excellent retirement-planning tool that provides a stream of income you cannot outlive.

The problem, however, is that annuities aren't always used appropriately. Worse, they aren't always sold appropriately by the annuity industry. Sales agents omit salient facts or smooth-talk unsophisticated buyers into investing in the wrong kind of annuity for all the wrong reasons—and those reasons always center around one thing: a fat commission. Like everything else on Wall Street, when it comes to annuities it pays to know what you're buying before you open your wallet.

Annuities come in two basic varieties: *fixed* and *variable,* which in turn can be either *immediate* or *deferred.*

Fixed annuities provide a fixed rate of return, much like a certificate of deposit. Earnings grow tax-deferred, meaning you will pay taxes on the profits at ordinary income rates when you withdraw the money. You have the option to take your money out of an annuity in a lump sum or to request that the annuity company pay you in fixed equal installments over some period of time, a process called annuitization. Once you annuitize your contract, you cannot alter it or request the remainder in a lump sum at some point.

Variable annuities provide a return that varies with the ups and downs of stock, bond, and money-market sub-accounts. These sub-accounts look and act like standard mutual funds;

you're in control of choosing how to invest your money across those sub-accounts, and you can switch your money around between whatever sub-accounts the insurer offers inside a particular variable annuity contract.

As with a fixed annuity, you can take a lump-sum payment or an annuity option. If you choose to annuitize, the payments can be either fixed or variable. Select the variable option, and your check can vary from one month to the next.

Immediate annuities begin to pay out a stream of income immediately or within a year. They're used to generate monthly income right now or in the very near future. Though the fixed rate of return is frequently similar to what you might find with a CD, the same amount of money invested in the annuity will provide a much larger amount of income than the CD will. That's because annuities return not just the investment income but a portion of your original principal, too.

The flip side of a larger monthly check is that when the annuity comes to an end, it will have no remaining value to offer you since you consumed it along the way. The CD will still have its original principal intact.

Deferred annuities have two phases: accumulation and distribution. In the accumulation phase, the annuity grows in size based on the underlying investment, be it a fixed rate of annual growth or a variable rate. If you withdraw the money during the accumulation phase, you are often penalized through so-called surrender charges (more on those momentarily).

In the distribution phase you reclaim your money either through a lump sum or regular annuity payments. You can choose to have the payout occur during some period of time you select, such as, say, twenty years, or over an indefinite period, meaning "for as long as you live." Assuming you opt to annuitize, the period you choose has a direct effect on the size of your monthly check. The shorter the period, the larger the income; the longer the period (and the lifetime income option is the longest), the smaller the check. The risk with a shorter payout period is that you can outlive your income. The risk with the longer payout period is that the income you generate might be insufficient for your needs.

Any profits withdrawn from a deferred annuity before you reach age 59½ are subject to a 10% penalty and are taxed as ordinary income.

Fixed-rate Immediate	Variable-rate Immediate
Pays a set rate of return, on par with what a CD might offer. Typically begins paying immediately or within a year. The payments generally do not change. Payments can last for a set number of years or be structured to provide income for life, no matter how long that is.	Pays a variable rate of return based on the performance of underlying investments. Pays out immediately or within the year. Payments can change based on the investment performance. Payments last for a set amount of years or for life.
Fixed-rate Deferred	**Variable-rate Deferred**
Has two phases: Pays a set rate of return during an accumulation phase that lasts for a prescribed number of years and then distributes the accumulated value during a payout phase that can last a set number of years or for life.	Has two phases: During accumulation phase, grows at a variable rate dependent on underlying investments in stocks and bonds. Distributes the accumulated value during a payout phase that can last a set number of years or for life.

With annuities there is no reason to save the punch line: Most investors are better off without an annuity and should simply stick with mutual funds.

Despite the flashy sales pitches, annuities can be a financial time bomb if you're not careful. State and federal regulators, including the Securities and Exchange Commission and the National Association of Securities Dealers, routinely punish brokers, agents, and financial services companies for shady annuity sales practices and routinely issue advisories alerting consumers to the dangers that annuities represent.

Because annuity sellers largely target retirees, who often

feel insecure about their finances to begin with, the most important warning to remember is this: For investors over the age of sixty-five, "annuities are probably **not** for you." The words in quotes—and the bold—comes from the Commonwealth of Massachusetts' securities division, which in 2005 distributed a pamphlet on annuity pitfalls after the state agency cracked down on inappropriate or dishonest annuity sales tactics in several high-profile incidents.

Consider some of the thornier problems you face with many annuities:

Taxes: On the surface, annuities seem tax friendly since their earnings grow tax-deferred. The reality is more complex and potentially damaging to your heirs. If you live long enough to begin drawing down your annuity, those earnings will be taxed as ordinary income, a rate that is typically higher than you'd pay on capital gains.

If you die first, the situation is even uglier for your heirs. At your death all the gains that accumulated through the years in your annuity are taxable to your heirs as ordinary income. By comparison, other investments, such as individual stocks, bonds, and mutual funds, have a step-up provision so that the value of the asset at your death becomes your heirs' original cost basis. In short, if your investment originally cost just $1 and it's worth $100,000 at your death, your heirs owe no taxes on all those profits. With an annuity, heirs pay taxes on every last penny of profit.

Thus, an annuity can create a potentially large and often unexpected tax obligation for heirs. If the profits are large enough, the taxes on the annuity could force heirs to sell off other assets in the estate (potentially creating a chain of taxable events) or have to dig into their own savings and investments to cover the costs. Pay very close attention to this when considering trading assets such as stocks, bonds, and mutual funds for an annuity because you're ultimately creating taxes where none exist.

Surrender Charges: These can be the most onerous aspect of an annuity. Worse, many annuity buyers don't realize these fees even exist.

Surrender charges are fees that annuity companies impose on you when you surrender your contract—that is, turn it back into the annuity company for the cash—before a certain period of time has elapsed. That surrender period—the time during which the surrender charge applies—can last from one year to fifteen years or more in some of the most egregious contracts. The charge itself is generally some percentage of the contract's value at the time you surrender it and can range from something small, like 1%, to something that borders on usurious, like 15% or more.

Surrender charges decline with time, typically at the rate of one percentage point per year. A contract with a 10% surrender charge might impose that charge over ten years, dropping the charge to 9% if you surrender the contract in the second year, 8% in the third year, and so on. Some contracts keep the maximum charge in place for several years before dropping it slowly. One example is an 8% charge that's in place for five years before it begins to ratchet down to 0% over the next eight years—a surrender period that extends a total of thirteen years.

Before buying any annuity, ask the salesperson about the size of the surrender charge and how long that charge remains in place. If you think there is any chance you might need access to your cash before the surrender period has run its course, you should avoid that annuity.

Fees and Expenses: Though there are certainly some very good, competitively priced annuities, most carry a host of fees that frequently are much more than you'd pay for other similar investments. Those fees and expenses erode your returns. Here are the types of fees you pay:

- Mortality and risk charges to cover the guaranteed death benefits that provide your heirs with a payout when you die, as with a life insurance policy.

- Administrative fees for back-office chores like record keeping.

- Fund expenses to pay the costs of the underlying mutual fund–like sub-accounts.

- Fees for special features built into annuities, such as guaranteed stepped-up benefits that automatically set the guaranteed death benefit at a higher level based on the performance of the sub-accounts; or principal protection, which insures that your heirs will never get back less than your original investment even if the investments ultimately underperform. All such features add additional costs to help the insurer compensate for the added risk it is assuming.

Why Buy an Annuity?

Since annuities can cause so many problems, you might wonder why anyone would ever own one. In many instances they shouldn't. However, in the right situation, the right kind of annuity can complement a nest egg for people already in retirement or provide a tax-deferred savings option for workers who still have many years left to save before they retire.

Retirees: Income, not accumulation, is the name of the game in retirement. For that reason, immediate annuities can be a smart investment for retirees—and far smarter than a variable annuity. Be warned, though, that salespeople try to foist variable annuities onto retirees because variable annuities generally offer larger commissions and more opportunities to convince retirees to use a so-called 1035 exchange to uselessly purchase a new annuity later.

An immediate annuity can create an assured base of income to supplement your Social Security checks and any other sources of income you might have. Moreover, immediate annuities with a lifetime payout option are particularly useful if you want assurances that your base of income will stay around for as long as you continue to live.

Variable annuities typically make little sense for retirees

BEWARE THE "1035 EXCHANGE"

IRS rules allow you to exchange one insurance contract for another without paying taxes on the first—a process called a 1035 exchange because of IRS Form 1035, which you must sign. Annuity salespeople are eager to convince you to exchange an old contract for a new contract, and most of the annuity sales that happen result from annuity salespeople persuading current annuity owners to exchange a perfectly fine annuity for a new contract. **Be very cautious before agreeing to a 1035 exchange.**

Ask yourself this question: Who benefits most from this transaction?

There can be good reasons to exchange contracts, such as buying a less expensive contract, one that offers certain guarantees that you might need, or one with a better range of investment options for you over the long haul. An exchange can also make sense if you're moving into a new contract where the surrender period is substantially shorter than the remaining surrender period on your current contract or where the underlying fees are dramatically lower than what you're currently paying. In that case, the cost savings over time will likely outweigh a surrender charge you might face, but you need to calculate that yourself to be sure.

For the most part, a 1035 exchange is a bad idea. Here's why:

- The seller is only after the commission.

- Trading your current annuity for a new one will typically subject you to a new, longer surrender period. Check your current contract; if you have fewer years remaining on the surrender period than the new contract would impose, don't switch unless there is a very compelling reason to do so.

- "Bonus" payments that a salesperson emphasizes on the new annuity are **not** a compelling reason to switch. Bonus payments work like this: The annuity company promises to add some amount, say 5%, to your account the moment you open it. That sounds like a sweet deal—you trade in a $100,000 annuity and you instantly have $105,000. But the reality is that your underlying fees on the new contract are more expensive or the surrender charge is more onerous, since the insurer is not simply giving you money for nothing. Moreover, the surrender penalty you must pay to exit the first contract could eat all or more of the bonus offered on the second contract. In short, you come out a loser, and the seller pockets several thousand dollars in commission.

Before you agree to exchange one annuity for another, ask the seller the questions below. If the answers don't convince you that you're the real winner in this transaction, then refuse to sign a 1035 exchange.

- How much will I lose from surrendering my current annuity? (You may need to call your current annuity company for that answer.)

- How long is the surrender period on the new contract, and what is the surrender schedule? (Compare this to the surrender period still remaining on your current contract.)

- What makes this new contract so compelling, and why do I need these new bells and whistles?

- How much do these new features cost? (Compare the underlying fees on your current annuity to the ones in the proposed annuity. The fees are spelled out in the prospectus, which you should ask for and hold on to. If you have trouble deciphering the language of the prospectus, have a friend or trusted advisor look over both prospectuses to help you better understand what you're getting into.)

- How are you being compensated or how much commission are you earning off this annuity? (If an agent ever tells you that you're paying no commission, kindly thank the agent for stopping by and escort him or her to the door. The agent is lying and not to be trusted. The only reason any broker or agent sells an investment product is to get paid. An agent who says you aren't paying anything is playing word games. While you may not pay a commission directly, you are paying it indirectly through the fees and charges you are subjected to.)

In short it comes down to this: Do not agree to a 1035 exchange unless you are positive that doing so will help your financial position.

because variable annuities are, first and foremost, accumulation products. Retirees generally don't have enough years to wait for the accumulation phase to end. Moreover, retirees generally don't have enough time to recoup mistakes from bad investments or a bad few years in the stock or bond market, which can shrivel the value of the underlying sub-accounts. Finally, the tax and surrender charge issues can wreak havoc on your finances or your heirs'.

The downside of most immediate annuities is that they typically don't adjust for inflation. The monthly check you get today will be the same monthly check you get twenty years from now, when costs will be more expensive. For that reason you should invest no more than about one-third of your assets in an annuity; the remainder of your money can grow in other accounts to offset the effects of inflation.

Workers: People still in the workforce are still in accumulation mode. Thus, they don't need the income of an immediate annuity but, rather, the tax-deferred growth potential of the stock and bond sub-accounts inside a variable annuity. But a variable annuity should be your last option.

Before investing in a variable annuity you should max out contributions to your company retirement savings plan and any IRA for which you might be eligible to contribute. Both of those offer tax savings; 401(k) contributions reduce your taxable income, while the IRA offers a tax deduction that can reduce the amount of money you owe the IRS each year. By contrast, a variable annuity, while it grows tax-deferred, offers no tax savings on your original contributions.

If you have maxed out your contributions in your employer's retirement savings plan and in an IRA, then sticking any excess income in a variable annuity can make sense. Variable annuities can also make sense for high-income couples who aren't eligible for IRA contributions but still want tax-deferred growth for another portion of their nest egg. Just be sure you have at least fifteen or twenty years remaining in the workforce so that you avoid surrender charges and allow the tax deferral to work as it's designed to.

Also, to keep your costs down and your returns up, go with a low-cost variable annuity provider such as TIAA-CREF (www.tiaa-cref.org) or Vanguard (www.vanguard.com). Both offer variable annuities with internal expenses below 1% of your account value annually. The average variable annuity is roughly three times that level.

Two Annuities to Beware Of

Annuity companies are forever tweaking their products in an effort to make them appear more tantalizing than they really are. Two in particular have become very popular, though once you understand how they work, you may want to think twice about buying them.

An **Equity-Indexed Annuity,** or EIA, is the love child of fixed and variable annuities. It has gained great popularity because it is frequently pitched as the safe, guaranteed alternative to investing in the stock market. No matter what, you earn a minimum guaranteed return (as with a fixed annuity), but the interest rate is linked to some stock market index (as with a variable annuity).

For most EIAs the underlying index is the Standard & Poor's 500, the leading broad-market U.S. stock index, though some shadow other indices. The overall effect essentially offers a floor you cannot fall below, along with an opportunity to participate in bigger stock market gains.

Yet EIAs can be very confusing investment contracts that aren't all they're marketed to be. State and federal regulators routinely caution investors to fully understand these products before investing because the gains that EIAs rack up depend entirely on a combination of underlying "indexing factors" built into each contract. The three factors below tend to be the most commonly used for determining the return you earn with an equity-indexed annuity:

- **Participation rates** determine how much of the gain from the underlying index will be credited to your annuity. That rate can vary from 100% to 60%. If the participation rate is, say, 70% and the index returns 10% for the year, your annuity is credited with just 7% (10×0.7).

- **Cap rates** put an upper limit on how much of the year's return will be credited to your account. If your cap rate is, say, 6% in any given year and the market is up 10% or 12% or 30%, you'll get only 6%. If the market is up 5%, you'll get 5%.

- **Spread or margin** sets a percentage-point amount that will be subtracted from the index's return. For instance, with a spread of 3% and an index return of 9%, your annuity would be credited with 6%.

These factors can be used in combination as well, so that in any given year you might get the spread, the cap, or the participation rate. If the spread on your EIA is 3%, the cap is 6%, and the participation rate is 70%, and the market's return for the year is 30%, well, you're not likely to get the 27% difference between the spread and the return or the 21% that would represent 70% of the return. Instead, you'll earn the 6%.

Even in situations where the participation rate is 100% of some index, the cap can limit you to a very small portion of that return. The upshot: You may not be participating in Wall Street as much as you're led to believe.

The second annuity to beware of is the **Bonus Annuity.** There's nothing quite like the lure of free money to get the greed surging through your veins. Bonus annuities play directly to that emotion.

With these annuities you receive a "bonus credit," a seemingly gracious addition to your deposit that the insurer seemingly offers as something of a "thank you for investing with us."

These credits typically amount to between 1% and 5% of your initial deposit. Start with $50,000 in a bonus annuity offering a 4% credit, and immediately you have $52,000. What's not to like about that?

A lot.

Insurance companies give away nothing for free, especially money. Bonus annuities typically have higher expenses than a similar nonbonus annuity, increasing your cost through the years and, in turn, lowering your overall profits. The added expenses show up in surrender charges that are higher, surrender periods that are longer, and internal fees and charges that are more onerous than those for the average annuity. And in what might be one of the more perverse examples of the industry's often duplicitous ways, some bonus annuities even impose an added fee designed specifically to cancel out over time the bonus you're paid up front. In effect, you paid yourself and ultimately you lose over time because the higher fee structure remains in place for the life of the contract.

Consider that $50,000 and suppose you have two options: a Traditional Variable Annuity that charges fees and expenses of 1.3% a year, and a Bonus Variable Annuity that gives you that 4% bonus up front but charges you 1.8% annually—a fairly normal fee differential. If both annuities generate the same 8% average annual return, the value of the Traditional Variable Annuity will surpass the Bonus Variable Annuity after the eighth year. After twenty years the Bonus Variable Annuity is worth $168,542, while the Traditional Variable Annuity holds $179,386. For accepting that extra 5% up front, you end up with 6% *less* than you would have if you had skipped the bonus to begin with.

With bonus annuities you also need to be aware that some insurers will, among other tactics, reclaim all or part of the bonus you were paid if you surrender the policy too soon or if you die and the insurer is forced to pay the death benefit to your beneficiaries.

Bonus annuities might sound like free money when the

ANNUITY RULES TO REMEMBER

Rule #1: Tax deferral generally will outweigh the additional costs of deferred annuities *only* if you hold the annuity as a long-term investment. Variable annuities in particular are notorious for high fees and commissions, and if you drop the contract within the first several years, you will invariably come out on the short end. If you can't invest in a deferred annuity for a decade or longer, don't invest in a deferred annuity.

Rule #2: Do not invest more than about one-third of your total liquid assets in an annuity. Annuities are highly illiquid, and if you need to get at your money in an emergency or for whatever reason, you will likely face a penalty. It is better to have the bulk of your liquid savings available to you in the event you ever need it.

Rule #3: An annuity purchased in an IRA or other tax-deferred account generally makes no sense. The IRA already offers tax-advantaged status, and the annuity will not give you additional tax advantages. In effect, the only thing you're doing is paying extra fees to own an annuity but getting no extra benefits for that.

Also, know that IRS rules require you to begin taking distributions from a traditional IRA when you hit age 70½—even if that would impose surrender charges on your annuity.

About the only time you might consider an annuity for an IRA is if your IRA is your only sizable investment account and you need or want a lifetime income option. Just make certain that you will own the contract long enough to avoid costly surrender penalties by the time you begin to withdraw the money.

Rule #4: Don't pay for what you don't need or want. Annuities come with a variety of bells and whistles designed to make them more appealing to investors. But nothing on Wall Street is free, and every bell and whistle has an underlying cost to the insurer. You can be sure that cost is built into the fees and expenses you're paying.

Also, never believe a seller who tells you that you're not paying a commission. You may not see any of your money go directly to the seller, but the insurance company is paying that agent on the back side—often 5% or more of the value of your contract. The cost of the commission is either built into the underlying annual fees you pay or there is a longer or larger surrender charge.

Rule #5: Most states impose a "free-look" period on annuity sales. Within that period, anywhere from ten days to a month, depending on the state, you have the right to cancel the contract for any reason—or no reason. Just call the insurer and say you want the contract voided, and you're entitled to get back every penny you invested.

Consumers who grow concerned within days of signing on for any annuity should cancel the contract. And, equally important, anyone concerned that an aged parent or family member might have been improperly sold an annuity should talk to that person about canceling the contract before it's too late.

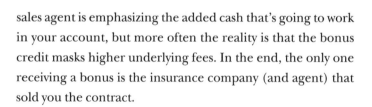

sales agent is emphasizing the added cash that's going to work in your account, but more often the reality is that the bonus credit masks higher underlying fees. In the end, the only one receiving a bonus is the insurance company (and agent) that sold you the contract.

HOME OWNER'S AND AUTOMOBILE INSURANCE

Life insurance insures your life; home owner's insurance and auto insurance insures your stuff. Nothing and no one requires that you buy life insurance, but home owner's and auto insurance policies are altogether different.

If you buy a house, a lender will mandate that you buy a home owner's policy. In fact, you won't be able to close on the purchase of a home unless you show proof of insurance, typically that you've already paid the first full year's premium.

Similarly, if you drive a car, you must have auto insurance—or you're breaking a law or two, given that nearly every state now requires proof that you carry some level of liability insurance.

Together, home owner's and automobile policies are known as "personal lines" of insurance. These mandatory policies aren't necessarily for your peace of mind, though they certainly provide that benefit. Instead, lenders require that your house be covered by a home owner's policy because that lender wants concrete assurance that if something ever happens to your home, you'll have enough money to repay the debt you owe. As for auto insurance, states mandate coverage because they have a vested interest in making sure that in the event you cause a wreck, you have money to pay for any damage to other cars and property or injuries to other people.

In both instances the benefit to you is apparent: You protect your assets to a certain degree because without insurance you would be on the hook for every dime if your house is damaged or if you total someone else's car.

So whether you call "home" the typical American suburban house, a mobile home, a duplex, a condominium, or a one-room cabin alongside a river or mountain, your dwelling and its contents need protection against damage caused by fire, tornado, water, mold, hail, burglary, or the liability of someone injuring himself on your property. And no matter whether your car is a high-end Italian roadster or a junker that smokes and chokes as it wheezes through town, your ride must be insured against the possibility that you will hurt someone else or damage their property.

HOME OWNER'S POLICIES

Your home is likely your most valuable possession, and you'd probably have trouble replacing it on your own in the event it was damaged or destroyed. The same holds for the possessions inside your home, which are also covered by your policy; individually you might be able to replace each one—at least financially if not necessarily emotionally. But in aggregate, could you rustle up enough cash to replace all of them at once?

For the amount of coverage you buy, home owner's insurance is a relative bargain, especially when compared to auto insurance. Insuring a home that costs several hundred thousand dollars can cost just several hundred dollars to $1,500 a year—frequently less than what you'd pay to insure an auto that might cost ten to twenty times less than your house. The reason: risk. Houses sit still; cars whiz about. And anything that moves is at a greater risk for causing damage. As a general rule, only about 10% of the risk in a home owner's policy comes from liability exposure—the possibility that someone is injured on your property. With a car, half the risk is the liability that your car will injure another person or property. Thus, cars are costlier to insure.

A home owner's policy provides varying levels of protection, the two most basic levels being:

- **Actual cash value:** Your home and its contents are covered up to their depreciated value. In practical terms this means that if you lose that console TV/record player that has dominated the family room since *Good Times* was a hot sitcom, the insurer will not be sending you a check large enough to afford a new flat-screen unit to hang on your wall. You'll be reimbursed an amount equal to what someone would pay to own a thirty-year-old television today, essentially a nominal amount.

- **Replacement cost:** Your home is insured so that even if the cost of rebuilding exceeds the amount of coverage you have, the insurer still pays the expenses. This once was a blanket guarantee. Even if you insured your home for $100,000 and it cost $700,000 to rebuild, the insurer picked up the tab. In some instances you can still buy such coverage, called "guaranteed replacement," but it's very pricey. More common today is a capped replacement cost. If you insure your house for, say, $250,000, the insurer will pay up to 20% to 25% more, or as much as $312,500, to replace your house. The size of the cap varies by insurer and state.

Most home owner policies provide for replacement cost coverage for your home and actual cash value coverage for your property. Be sure you know what cap the insurer imposes so that you'll know the true limits of your coverage if ever you need to rebuild your home.

Taking Stock of What You Own

If a tornado, fire, or hurricane obliterated your home, would you be able to make a list of everything you owned? Could you do it fairly quickly so that you could file a claim as soon as possible with your insurer? Finally, would you be able to prove you lost what you say you lost?

As much of a hassle as this task is, taking an inventory of all that you own may one day serve you well. ✎ *page 54* Knowing what you own also serves another purpose—it allows you to better tailor your insurance needs. Your possessions might be insured for, say, $50,000, but you might find that their true value is $80,000. And you might realize you have certain items, such as a high-quality coin collection, high-dollar jewelry, or extensive camera or computer gear, that your standard policy doesn't cover fully. In that case you'll need extended coverage, a so-called endorsement, that provides adequate protection for these possessions at an additional cost.

A proper inventory includes a list of items—delineated by rooms—that makes note of any model and serial numbers, the original cost, and the original purchase date. To the degree possible, it's wise to keep the original receipt as well. As proof of your ownership, video what you own—including a close-up on the brand, model, and serial number where applicable. Keep the list of items and the tape in a fireproof box, a home safe, or a safe-deposit box at the bank.

Catch a C.L.U.E.

The insurance industry not only keeps track of you, it keeps track of your house. Through something called a C.L.U.E. Personal Property report, insurers know how many claims have been paid on a particular house, how much those claims have cost, and what types of damages have been reimbursed. (C.L.U.E. is the acronym for Comprehensive Loss Underwriting Exchange.)

Anyone looking to buy a home might want to take a peek at a C.L.U.E. report, too, since insurers can and do deny coverage based not just on your claims history but that of the house you want. With a C.L.U.E. report you might discover that a home you're interested in has a history of water or mold damage—a red flag that many insurers shy away from because of the costs associated with remediation. That's a house you might want to steer clear of, lest you find out after you've already bought it that insurers want nothing to do with your house or will offer coverage only at elevated rates.

Home owners have a right to a copy of the C.L.U.E. report on their property; those reports are available online at www.choicetrust.com (under the Consumer Solutions tab) or by calling 866-312-8076. Buyers don't have a legal right to view the C.L.U.E. report on a property they're interested in purchasing. However, you can—and should—request that the current home owner provide it before you agree to buy the house.

How Much Home Owner's Insurance Is Enough?

That question seems like a no-brainer. You insure your house for the purchase price or, at the very least, what you owe the mortgage company.

Of course that could be a disaster. Consider these two examples:

1. You just bought a new house that was built as part of a brand-new neighborhood. The house cost $200,000, and you insure it for the full value.

Chances are that's not enough.

Builders who build numerous houses in a neighborhood buy materials in bulk, and they pay for labor basically in bulk. When they're slapping together dozens of houses all at once, it's substantially cheaper than if they build a single home. Yet if something destroys your house, your otherwise cookie-cutter home suddenly becomes a custom home. And buying materials and paying for labor for a custom home is always more expensive. Alas, the cost of rebuilding may well exceed that $200,000.

REMEMBER

The cost to rebuild your house may be well below the purchase price in many expensive housing markets. That's because of the land. In a place like New York City, the land is far more valuable than the dilapidated brownstone sitting on it. You do not need to insure the land, since even in a disaster that dirt remains even if your home doesn't.

If you buy a $600,000 house, using a $500,000 mortgage, yet rebuilding that house would cost only $300,000, there's no reason to insure the entire purchase price. In fact, most insurance companies won't let you. That's a risk mitigation measure because insurers have no interest in providing an incentive for a home owner to insure a property for $600,000, *accidentally* torch the place, claim the $600,000 loss, rebuild for $300,000, and pocket the difference.

Nevertheless, a lender might tell you that you must purchase enough insurance to cover your mortgage. In truth, many states impose laws that say lenders cannot force you to insure more than the cost necessary to rebuild your home. Home owners in states with outsized housing costs often don't realize this and pay too much for coverage. Savvy consumers know to resist such a push by a lender and will use their state's laws as support.

2. You buy that same house for $200,000 and fully insure it, and you've lived in the house for a decade or so. If your home is destroyed, you may discover you are woefully underinsured because chances are good that you haven't increased your coverage based on the escalating value of your home.

During the ten years that you've lived in your house, home prices in your area may have risen 3% annually, on par with historical housing price increases. Your $200,000 home now has a market value of $361,000. Moreover, the cost of building a home—from materials to labor—has increased, too. With a $200,000 payout you might have to build or buy a smaller home, or dig into your savings to come up with the difference.

The best bet for making sure you buy appropriate coverage for your house is to ask a local contractor, real-estate agent, or insurance agent what rebuilding costs would run for your particular style of house, based on your home's square footage and the interior finish you have. This way you can be certain you're not paying for too much coverage or are underinsuring your biggest asset.

AUTOMOBILE POLICIES

Your house is your biggest expense. Your car is your biggest liability.

While your house isn't likely to run over a pedestrian, there's a chance your car could do just that while you're monkeying around trying to tune in to a favored station on your new satellite radio. In the legal world those sorts of incidents routinely rack up damage awards of $500,000 to $1 million or more, depending on the severity of the injuries. With so many ways to wreak havoc, little wonder that cars are the biggest liability and why it is that auto liability coverage can be so expensive.

Auto insurance is often the first consumer-insurance contract we become familiar with. The minute we learn to drive as teenagers, parents put us on their policy—and we promptly jack up their rates by speeding into a moving violation, backing into a parked car, or rear-ending the vehicle in front of us at the light.

Auto insurance is essentially a series of individual policies packaged together in one contract. To gain a better understanding of what it is you actually own, it helps to know what protections these individual policies provide. In general there are about seven main protections a typical auto policy covers, though not all states mandate each of them.

- **Liability** is the most important component of any auto policy. Liability coverage pays for damages to property and injuries to people that you cause. States typically require a minimum amount of liability coverage, though what that level is varies from one state to the next. While the minimum is prescribed, you can—and probably should—carry more than the minimum to protect your other assets against a lawsuit in the event you seriously injure or kill someone while driving.

- **Collision** is the insurance that covers damage to your vehicle caused by you or another driver—or another object if you run into, say, a tree or lamppost. It is smart to carry collision on a new car, but if your car is old and not worth more than about $2,000, there's no compelling reason to pay for collision coverage.

- **Comprehensive** pays for loss or damages that don't result from a wreck. This would include incidents such as a tree falling on your car, a thief stealing your vehicle, or damage caused by fire, hail, or water. Again, if your car isn't worth much, you can skip this coverage to save a little money— maybe to buy a new car?

- **Uninsured motorist** coverage pays for the damages wrought upon your car by another motorist who doesn't carry liability insurance.

- **Underinsured motorist** is very similar to uninsured motorist coverage because it pays for damages to your car that go beyond the liability coverage carried by the driver who ran into you.

- **Medical** provides for medical expenses that stem from a car wreck, regardless of who is at fault. The coverage extends to the insured driver as well as anyone the insured driver injures in an auto accident.

- **Personal Injury Protection,** or PIP, pays medical expenses for the insured driver only, regardless of who is at fault in the wreck. Some states require PIP protection; others don't.

State laws determine what level of liability insurance you're required to carry if you drive. If you carry only the minimum, rest assured that attorneys for anyone you injure seriously in an auto accident will almost assuredly go after any other assets you might have. That is why it's smarter to pay a few extra dollars each year to buy a greater level of protection that can shield your personal assets.

In some ways what you ultimately pay for auto insurance is a bit like a buffet you might find in a New York City deli: You can pick whatever you want and in whatever quantity, and then you pay based on what your selections weigh. You might choose minimal collision coverage, for instance, but really pile on the liability coverage in order to protect your savings. You might increase your medical coverage and then increase your deductible to lower your overall cost.

Auto insurance is often quoted based on the liability maximums that the policy will pay, something like 50/100/20.

The 50 represents the maximum $50,000 in liability coverage for bodily injury that your insurer will pay to people you injure in an accident. If the cost of the medical bills, lost wages, and pain and suffering exceeds $50,000, then you are responsible for the difference. This covers only other people, not you, and is a per-person amount. So if you injure two people, each is entitled to a maximum of $50,000.

The 100 represents the cumulative total of $100,000 in bodily injuries that your insurer will pay out per accident. Thus, if you injure three people and their combined medical bills exceed $100,000, you're on the hook for the remainder.

The 20 represents $20,000 in liability coverage for someone else's property that you damage in an auto accident. This is a cumulative dollar amount that your insurer will pay to replace the cars and other property you damage or destroy in a wreck you cause. Also, this is the total the insurer will pay per accident, not per person. If you cause a three-car accident that totals two other cars, your insurer will stop paying once $20,000 in damages is reached. Anything beyond that comes out of your pocket.

Pay attention to the quote that an insurance agent gives you. Auto insurance, unlike home owner's insurance, is typically quoted in six-month intervals, not yearlong intervals. You'll need to double the quote to know what you're paying annually. And shop around, making sure to check in with direct-to-consumer agencies you find online, such as Geico. com, Progressive.com, and others. Because there are no agents in the middle requiring salaries or commissions, you'll typically find more favorable rates. Aggregators such as InsWeb. com provide quotes from several different insurers, allowing you to do some comparison shopping.

If you are a high-risk driver—one who has multiple tickets or accidents on your driving record—you might consider using an insurance broker who can price policies for you across multiple insurance companies, including many that you might not be aware of that are willing to take on higher risks.

How Much Auto Insurance Is Enough?

As noted above, many states mandate the absolute minimum coverage you must carry in order to even back out of your driveway. It is wiser, though, to purchase much broader coverage as a way of protecting yourself and your assets from an overly litigious lawyer trying to recoup millions of dollars for a driver you might have injured only marginally in a minor fender bender.

Many motorists—typically between 25% and 40%, depending on the insurer—choose to buy the state-required minimum coverage, viewing the purchase of auto insurance as a necessary evil. If you can afford more, the protection is worth the expense, given the tremendous financial liability you would face in the event you caused bodily harm to someone in a wreck. If you have any assets, a plaintiff's attorney will go after them, including possibly the forced sale of your home if the injuries are grievous enough.

How much coverage is enough? Well, what amount of financial assets do you have at risk? Prudence says you should insure what you stand to lose if you can afford to.

If that much insurance is too pricey—even with a higher deductible—then at least go as high as your finances will allow. In general, "minimum" coverage is whatever your particular state deems the lowest amount of liability insurance you must carry. "Regular" coverage typically pays liabilities up to $50,000 per person and $100,000 per accident. "Premium" coverage goes up to $100,000 per person and $300,000 per accident. And "ultra" coverage is $300,000/$300,000 or, with some insurers, $250,000/$500,000. Various insurers use different designations for the various types of coverage—such as *ultra* and *premium*—but the liability limits are generally the same.

GOOD CREDIT = LOWER INSURANCE RATES

Though an obvious connection seems strained, what you pay for your insurance depends not just on the factors listed above but also on the good, the bad, and the atrocious inside your credit report.

Insurance companies say their claims experiences through the years show that consumers who are conscientious with their dollars tend to be better risks when it comes to insurance because they file fewer claims. Folks who don't manage their finances well tend to be worse risks. They often struggle financially and are likely to file more claims since they don't have the income or the savings to cover even the small losses. And although some insurance commissioners argue that using credit reports to help set insurance premiums is wrong, the insurance industry widely relies on this practice to create an insurance score that helps determine the premium you'll pay.

So the lower your credit score, the higher your rates; and the higher your credit score, the lower your rates.

By law an insurer must inform you if it factors your credit score into your premium calculation. As a rule, ask your insurer if it pulled your credit score and, if so, how your score affected your premium. This is also a perfect time to pull a copy of your credit score yourself to be sure that there are no errors that might otherwise push you into a category that is unnecessarily more expensive.

DON'T FILE DINKY CLAIMS OR TOO MANY CLAIMS

Your son is mowing the lawn, and a rock rockets through your sliding-glass door, a $500 expense. Someone breaks into your car and filches your new $250 CD changer. Who do you call?

If you call your insurance company to file a claim, you could be making a big mistake that ultimately will cost you much more than the price tag on that shattered window.

Consumers wrongly assume that because they're paying for an insurance policy, they're going to get their money's worth by filing claims for every niggling incident that happens, be it that rock through the window, a busted water heater, or a small-time burglary. That's not what insurance is designed to cover.

Insurance protects you specifically at those times when a loss is truly substantial, when it would create a definite financial hardship, or when it is catastrophic. A roof shredded by hail, a home gutted by fire, or a car totaled in an accident—these are the times you want to file an insurance claim because the expense is generally more than most people would be able to cover from their savings and other assets.

The insurance industry keeps track of how often you file claims and the nature of those claims. File too many dinky or marginal claims, and your insurer can—and likely will—drop you. Additionally, other insurers will be inclined to deny coverage when you go hunting for new insurance. If you do find a new insurer willing to take you on, you will almost assuredly be dumped into the high-risk pool, meaning you'll pay much steeper rates.

Ultimately, that relatively small claim to recoup the cost of your smashed patio window or pilfered CD player could end up costing you substantially more in premium payments, not to mention the frustration of finding a new insurance carrier.

If you have a legitimate claim, by all means file it. For small claims, however, show restraint. To protect yourself you should be self-insured against small occurrences by building into your savings an amount of money you can draw on to cover the occasional losses that you'd otherwise be tempted to slough off onto your insurance company.

What defines "too many small claims" isn't universal; different insurers tolerate different levels of claims activity. And depending on how aggressively a particular insurer is pursuing new business at any given point, the company may not be bothered by a string of claims or will at least still be interested in offering you coverage.

But here's what too many claims can do to your costs: File one claim, and your premium can rise between 25% and 35%, depending on the state in which you live. File a second claim within three years, and your premium could go up another 35% to 40%. File a third claim within three years, and you can tack on an additional 40%—and you risk losing coverage. If you manage to keep your policy, what might have cost $1,500 a year can now cost nearly $4,000 after three claims.

RULE TO REMEMBER

If you ever receive a nonrenewal notice from your insurer, don't wait until your policy lapses to find new coverage. Insurers must give you at least thirty days' notice before terminating your policy, sometimes sixty days depending on the state. Start shopping for new insurance immediately so you can honestly tell an agent you still have coverage. If you wait until you're officially dropped, an insurer could require a much higher premium or deny coverage altogether.

If you are dropped or denied coverage, you have the right to receive a copy of your claims history by visiting www.consumerdisclosure.com.

LOWERING THE COST OF INSURANCE

Insurers offer numerous way to trim the costs of a home owner's or auto policy. Buying both policies from the same insurer, for instance, will typically cut your costs by 15% or 20%.

Here are some other ways to economize.

For home owners:

- Place deadbolt locks on all doors.

- Have an automatic sprinkler system in the home.

- Install a burglar alarm and/or fire-detection system that is centrally monitored.

- Have fire extinguishers in the home.

- Use smoke detectors.

- Stop smoking because some insurers offer nonsmoker discounts.

- Allow an interior inspection. Some insurers now offer a discount of 10% to 15% if, at the time the policy is underwritten, you allow an insurance inspector to inspect the inside of your home, looking for potential hazards to avoid problems before they occur—even little things like changing the water hose connectors on the washing machine from plastic to metal to prevent cracks and thus a water damage claim from leaks.

For drivers:

- Insure all cars with the same company for a multi-car discount.

- Avoid tickets. Many insurers offer good-driver discounts if you have a clean driving record for three to five years.

- Install antitheft devices such as a LoJack system or have your vehicle identification number (VIN) etched on all the windows, making those pieces of glass less attractive to thieves who otherwise want to sell them.

- Buy cars and trucks with antilock brakes and restraint systems such as airbags.

- For teens, completing a young driver's education program, generally offered by all the major insurers, can knock 15% or 20% off Mom and Dad's insurance.

- Smart young drivers are also eligible for cheaper rates. Those who make the dean's list or have excellent grades are often a better risk.

- For older drivers, completing a defensive driving course can reduce your premiums.

- If you allow your insurer to electronically draw your premium out of your checking account, you may be eligible for a discount.

- Become a mathematician, scientist, or engineer. Statistically speaking, certain professions have proven over time to present a reduced risk, and insurers reward that with lower premiums. Ask your insurer if it offers discounts for certain careers and what those careers are. You might be eligible for cheaper rates based on what you do for a living.

- Do not duplicate coverage. If you have towing or rental coverage through the American Automobile Association or through some dealer plan with the purchase of your new car, you can cut those coverages from your auto insurance policy and save money.

Finally, whether it is auto insurance or a home owner's policy, shop around. This is the single best way to lower your premiums because if you visit twenty different insurance companies, you can come away with twenty different quotes.

And once you have coverage, don't assume it's the best you can get year in and year out. People grow complacent and just pay their premiums out of habit or because they loathe the thought of having to shop for insurance. But every few years you should shop your policies again to see if you can find lower premiums or better coverage for the same price. Remember that there are more than one thousand insurance companies selling auto and home policies; you're bound to find affordable prices somewhere.

CHAPTER 7

TAXES

When was the last time you flushed the toilet?

When was the last time you walked on the sidewalk . . . drove on the street . . . threw a ball in the park . . . hopped on a bus or subway . . . sent your kids to public school . . . called on the police or fire department for some emergency, real or imagined . . . relied on a crosswalk to cross a busy highway while a red traffic light kept at bay drivers in a rush?

The everyday utilities and services we use by rote come from the taxes that we, as taxpayers, pay to our counties, cities, states, and the federal government. Sure, we gripe while doing so because of the sometimes shockingly profligate ways of politicians who would never run their family budgets so dismally. Nevertheless, despite the waste, lots of tax dollars go to making life safer, more convenient, and more enjoyable.

It all starts with your paycheck.

PAYROLL TAXES

As anyone earning a paycheck has no doubt noticed, taxes shrink your income every payday. Collectively, these deductions are the "payroll taxes" siphoned from all workers' paychecks to fund federal programs such as Social Security and Medicare. In most states you also pay state income taxes; that's not true everywhere because eight states don't impose taxes on their residents—though you might still face certain municipal taxes and maybe even a commuter tax.

The tax system takes a pay-as-you-earn approach, deducting throughout the course of the year proportional pieces of your overall tax obligation. The logic is sound: Workers, left to their own devices, would likely spend the money during the year and have nothing left to pay a big lump sum of taxes come April 15, the annual date that federal and most state taxes are due.

THE TAX MAN
DOESN'T COMETH

States that don't collect state income taxes:

Alaska

Florida

Nevada

South Carolina

Tennessee

Texas

Washington

Wyoming

Note: Florida collects an Intangible Personal Property Tax; Tennessee taxes interest and dividend income only.

Of course, paychecks aren't the only sources of income taxed before you see the money. If you have ever won a jackpot of more than $1,200 playing the slot machines or some other game of chance, you know the casino automatically withholds taxes before giving you your winnings. Pension payments and bonuses likewise have taxes taken out before making it into your hands, as does income from annuities, sick pay, unemployment compensation, and taxable fringe benefits such as moving costs an employer might pay to relocate you. In some situations you might even have to pay taxes on your Social Security check as a retiree.

All of this money goes to the Internal Revenue Service in your name so that when you file your Form 1040 tax return every year, the government knows how much you've paid into the system through the months. If it's too much, you get back the overpayment. If it's too little, you'll need to write a check to cover the difference.

THE W-4 FORM

How much money your employer ultimately deducts from your paycheck depends on how you fill out your W-4 Form, which you do on your first day at a new job. Through this form you tell your employer essentially how much money to withhold from each paycheck to cover the taxes you'll need to pay for the year. The withholding amount is based on the number of exemptions you claim for dependents. Each exemption reduces the amount of money withheld.

Of course, if you fib on the W-4, it catches up with you at the end of the year when you file your tax return and find that you owe a ton of money. Plus, just so you don't do it again, if you underwithhold by too large an amount the taxes you ultimately owe, the IRS charges you interest on the money you should have sent in along the way. If you're really egregious about it, the agency can penalize you and pursue criminal charges for intentionally falsifying a W-4 to reduce or eliminate the taxes your employer must otherwise withhold.

Filling out a W-4 can seem complicated, and many people just hope they're doing it right. Folks too often opt for the lowest number of exemptions, and thus the maximum withholding, just to be sure they don't owe taxes at the end of the year or to ensure they get money back, as though a tax refund is an unexpected windfall from the government. In reality it is your money all along; you worked for it. If you're the altruistic type, there's nothing wrong with letting the government hang on to the cash during the year and use it for government needs; you'll get it back, certainly, but you won't have earned a dime because the government doesn't pay any interest on the use of your cash. It is better to have access to the money yourself during the year for your own needs or to save. If nothing else, it's cash that will flow through your spending plan that you can allocate to paying down any debt.

PaycheckCity.com offers a range of free paycheck-related calculators, including a W-4 assistant that can help you

WHO'S FICA AND WHY IS FICA TAKING MY MONEY?

Under the Federal Insurance Contributions Act, known simply as FICA, you must pay 12.4% of your earned income into the Old Age Survivors and Disability Insurance account (OASDI), also known as the Social Security system, the safety net begun in January 1937 by President Franklin D. Roosevelt to ensure that every retiree has a basic level of income to live on. You pay another 2.9% into the Medicare system to ensure that retirees have basic medical needs covered.

Your employer pays half the bill, or 7.65% of your pay (6.2% for Social Security, 1.45% for Medicare). The Social Security portion is subject to an income limit, which in 2005 was $90,000. If you earn more than that, the portion above $90,000 is not subject to OASDI taxes. However, it is subject to Medicare taxes, which have no earned-income limit.

❦

determine how much you should really be withholding, based on your income and the deductions you're likely to have for the year. The IRS Web site also offers a withholding calculator. Have a recent pay stub handy, though; you'll need it.

Remember that your W-4 is not a static document. You don't fill it out on your first day of work and forget about it forever. If your life changes, your W-4 should change, too. If you get married or divorced during the year, have a child or adopt one, or can no longer claim a child or someone else as a dependent, then you should recalibrate your W-4. All of these changes will alter the taxes you ultimately owe, and you don't want to find out at tax time that you didn't withhold enough money or that you withheld too much.

EXEMPTIONS

These are amounts you get to deduct immediately from your taxable income, lowering your tax burden. You automatically get an exemption for yourself as well as one for your spouse if you are married and one for each child or dependent who relies on your earnings for support. In 2005, exemptions were worth $3,200 for you, your spouse, and each qualifying dependent.

There are rules for claiming exemptions on dependents; you can't just make up a kid or twelve to lower your taxes. For one thing, you'll need a valid Social Security number, so forget about claiming the dog. At high-income levels—$218,950 as a couple in 2005—the exemption begins to phase out.

THE W-2 FORM

This is the skeleton around which your annual tax return is built. By January 31 of every year your employer mails to you your W-2 Form. You'll receive three copies: Part A goes with your state tax return, Part B goes with your federal return, and Part C remains in your files. (If you're self-employed, you won't receive a W-2 but instead will report your income from Form 1099, on Schedule C, or Schedule F if you're a farmer.)

Among other entries on the W-2 is how much money you earned during the previous year in salary, bonuses, and reported tips, as well as how much your employer withheld in various taxes and any employer-sponsored retirement savings plan contributions you made.

When your W-2 arrives, make sure the information is accurate and that your name and, in particular, your Social Security number don't contain any errors. More than likely the IRS will note an error on your return and send it back for you to correct before processing your taxes.

If something has changed in your life—perhaps you

THE W-2 FORM

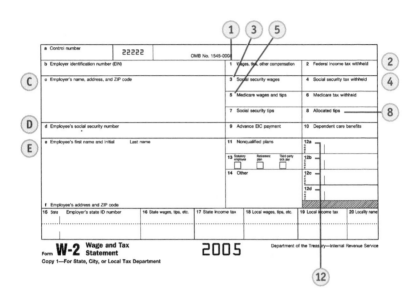

Form **W-2** Wage and Tax Statement **2005** Department of the Treasury—Internal Revenue Service

Copy 1—For State, City, or Local Tax Department

Boxes C, D, and E: Make sure the information in these boxes is accurate, especially your Social Security number in Box D. A wrong Social Security number can cause glitches in your return or incorrectly credit your earnings to someone else. The problems can be fixed, but it's easier to fix it on the front end.

Boxes 1, 2, 3, and 4: Make sure these accurately reflect your earnings and federal and Social Security taxes withheld, because they have an impact not just on how much you owe in taxes but the calculation of how much you're eligible to receive in Social Security payments one day.

Take special note of Box 3: Social Security stops taxing wages at a certain level ($90,000 in 2005). You want to be sure this number does not mistakenly exceed the income cap for a given year. If it does, you may have been overtaxed as well in Box 4. Also, if you earn more than the annual salary cap, Boxes 1 and 3 should not match.

Box 8: If you have an amount in this box, you'll need to add it to the amount in Box 1 and report it as additional compensation. You'll also have to complete IRS Form 4137, which will require you to pay additional Social Security and Medicare taxes on this lump of money.

Box 12: If there's a number here, there will be a code associated with it to explain what the sum is for. This is a brief explanation of the various codes:

A. Uncollected Social Security on tips.

B. Uncollected Medicare tax on tips.

C. Cost of group term life insurance greater than $50,000, included in your wages.

D. Elective deferrals into a 401(k) cash or deferred compensation plan, or a Thrift Savings Plan.

E. Elective deferrals into section 403(b) plans.

F. Elective deferrals under a section 408(k)(6) salary reduction.

G. Elective deferrals and employer contributions into a section 457(b) deferred compensation plan.

H. Elective deferrals into a Section 501(c)(18)(D) tax-exempt organization plan.

J. Nontaxable sick pay.

K. 20% excise tax on excess golden parachute payments.

L. Substantiated employee business expense reimbursements (nontaxable).

M. Uncollected Social Security on taxable cost of group term life insurance more than $50,000 (former employees only).

N. Uncollected Medicare tax on taxable cost of group term life insurance greater than $50,000 (former employees only).

P. Excludable moving expense reimbursements paid directly to employees (not included in other boxes).

R. Employer contributions to an Archer Medical Savings Account.

S. Employee salary reduction contributions under a section 408(p).

T. Adoption benefits (not included in Box 1). You must also complete Form 8839, Qualified Adoption Expenses.

V. Income from exercise of nonstatutory stock option(s).

recently married and your name on your Social Security card no longer matches the name on your W-2—there is always the chance that the IRS will alter your return without sending it back to you, changing your marital status to reflect what is in its records and adjusting your refund accordingly. You will be able to fix any snafus, of course, but why go through that bother when you can prevent them in the first place?

Although your employer, by law, must provide you with a W-2, that doesn't always happen. Maybe the form is lost in the mail; maybe your employer closed shop. Whatever the case, you still must file your tax returns on time—by April 15—even if you never receive your form. The IRS can help you with Form 4852, which is a substitute W-2. To make it easier on you just in case, save your last pay stub of the year or the last pay stub you receive when leaving an employer because you never know if that company will go out of business during the year.

INCOME TAXES

To understand the way income taxes work, you need to know the tax rates. This is what federal tax rates looked like in 2004 for taxpayers filing their returns in 2005. Find your filing status—single, married filing jointly, etc.—and then scroll down to locate your income range. Look to the far left, and that's your tax rate.

Tax Rate	Single Filers	Married Filing Jointly or Qualifying Widow/ Widower	Married Filing Separately	Head of Household
10%	Up to $7,150	Up to $14,300	Up to $7,150	Up to $10,200
15%	$7,151 to $29,050	$14,301 to $58,100	$7,151 to $29,050	$10,201 to $38,900
25%	$29,051 to $70,350	$58,101 to $117,250	$29,051 to $58,625	$38,901 to $100,500
28%	$70,351 to $146,750	$117,251 to $178,650	$58,626 to $89,325	$100,501 to $162,700
33%	$146,751 to $319,100	$178,651 to $319,100	$89,326 to $159,550	$162,701 to $319,100
35%	$319,101 or more	$319,101 or more	$159,551 or more	$319,101 or more

In this case "income" doesn't refer to your salary. What you owe in taxes is based on your "adjusted gross income," known as AGI. In simple terms—and there's nothing simple about the U.S. tax code—AGI represents all the income you earned during the year from salary, dividends, interest, reportable gambling winnings, tips, and the like, minus the larger of your standard or itemized deductions. Your AGI is the number that drives just about everything on your federal Form 1040 tax return every year.

Not all income is taxable, however. You might recall from the Investing section that interest paid on municipal bonds isn't taxable at the state, local, or federal level. Nor are the contributions taxable that you make to an employer-sponsored retirement savings plan, such as a 401(k), or to an Individual Retirement Account. For that reason taxpayers looking to reduce their tax bill, while at the same time doing more to prepare for retirement, should fund their retirement accounts as fully as possible. High-income earners, meanwhile, are often well served by mixing a healthy dose of municipal bonds into their portfolio because the income probably won't push you into an even higher tax bracket.

Life insurance death payouts also generally escape taxation, as do damage claims arising from stolen or destroyed property.

Standard Deduction: This is a preset deduction for taxpayers who don't have many individual tax deductions to claim. The IRS says about two-thirds of all taxpayers use the standard deduction. It is certainly easy; there are no additional complicated forms and worksheets to fill out. For 2004 the standard deduction for a single filer was $4,850, and it was $9,700 for married couples filing a joint tax return.

In the simplest of terms, if you're married and you and your spouse earn a combined $65,000, and you have no other income and no other deductions, you'd take the standard deduction of $9,700 and, voilà, your AGI is $55,300—putting you in the 15% tax bracket.

Itemized Deductions: These represent the cumulative value of various individual deductions you claim on your tax return, on Schedule A. You can take deductions for all manner of items, such as medical expenses, property taxes paid during the year, interest expense you paid on, say, a mortgage, charitable contributions, unreimbursed job costs, moving expenses, and so on. Some deductions have certain caveats; for example, your medical costs must equal at least 7.5% of your AGI before you can claim it. With moving expenses you must relocate for work, and the distance between your new job and your former residence must be at least fifty miles longer than your former commute.

Though itemizing can be a time-consuming chore, it pays to exert the effort if the total amount of your items exceeds your standard deduction. The itemized list will lower the taxes you owe, meaning a smaller check for you to write to the government or a bigger check that Uncle Sam will send you.

State and Local Sales Taxes

Instead of itemizing all your deductions, the IRS, beginning with tax year 2004, started allowing taxpayers to instead deduct on their federal tax returns the state and local sales taxes they paid during the year instead of state and local income taxes.

You have to choose, though; you can't deduct sales taxes and income taxes. For that reason you'll need to calculate which option is more valuable. For residents of those eight states without state sales taxes, this is an easy decision.

You have two ways to claim the sales tax deduction: If you don't keep all your receipts, you can use a computational method to calculate a deduction by downloading IRS Publication 600 from the IRS Web site. That publication will walk you through a worksheet based on what state you live in.

If you do keep all your receipts, then you can tally the cumulative sales tax you paid during the year. The resulting number is the size of your deduction. Now, just to ensure you take the largest deduction, also do the computational method to make sure it's not bigger; if it is, use the computational method instead.

There are some caveats to be aware of if you choose the taxes-paid option instead of the computational method. You can only deduct the actual sales tax you paid or your state's general sales tax rate, whichever is smaller. For instance, if your state charges a general sales tax of 6% but the sales tax imposed on clothes is 3%, then you can only deduct the $3 in taxes that you actually paid on that $100 shirt—not $6. Similarly, if your state taxes new cars at 8%, you can only deduct $600 paid on that $10,000 truck you bought, not the $800 you actually paid.

MARGINAL AND EFFECTIVE TAX RATES

Income tax rates work by taxing your income at different levels as your income progresses up the scale. Just because you're a single taxpayer with an AGI of, say, $100,000, doesn't mean you owe $28,000 in taxes because you fall into the 28% tax bracket. Only your highest dollar of income is taxed at the highest level; this is what's known as your *marginal tax rate*. Your income is actually taxed at each level along the way. So with that $100,000, the first $7,150 is taxed at 10%, the next $21,900 (or $29,050, the top end of the 15% range, minus the $7,150 already taxed at the 10% level) is taxed at 15%, and so on. Ultimately, it looks like this:

Tax Rate	Single Filers	Taxable Income	Taxes Due
10%	Up to $7,150	$ 7,150	$ 715
15%	$7,151 to $29,050	$ 21,900	$ 3,285
25%	$29,051 to $70,350	$ 41,300	$10,325
28%	$70,351 to $146,750	$ 29,650	$ 8,302
	Totals	$100,000	$22,627

In all, this taxpayer would owe taxes totaling $22,627, resulting in an *effective tax rate* of 22.63%.

TAX CREDITS VERSUS TAX DEDUCTIONS

What's better: a credit or a deduction?

The question might sound like semantics, but a credit is always better. A credit is a dollar-for-dollar subtraction from your total federal tax bill. A deduction, meanwhile, lowers the taxes you owe by a certain percentage—that percentage being whatever marginal tax rate you fall into. Here is how it looks in a simplified fashion:

TAX DEDUCTION VERSUS TAX CREDIT

Example for someone in the 25% tax bracket.

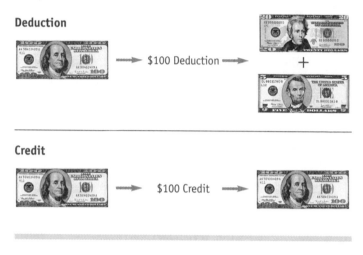

Deduction

$100 Deduction

+

Credit

$100 Credit

TABLE A

	Tax Deduction		
Tax deduction	Tax rate		Tax savings
$100 ×	25%	=	$25

TABLE B

	Tax Credit	
Tax deduction		Tax savings
$100	=	$100

Basically it comes down to this: A credit reduces your tax bill; a deduction reduces the amount of income that is taxed.

LOWERING YOUR TAXES

The Holy Grail of taxpayers. The possibilities for lowering your taxes are enormous and depend entirely on your activities for the year. If you start a home-based business, there are home-office deductions and, possibly, travel expenses. If you adopt a child, you're eligible for an adoption tax credit. If you move

THE AMT: AMERICA'S SECRET TAX

If death and taxes are the only assurances, it may well be that the AMT kills everyone.

The AMT, or Alternative Minimum Tax, is essentially a parallel tax code that the IRS enforces and that is designed to keep wealthy taxpayers from shirking their tax obligations by employing sophisticated tax shelters. Basically, taxpayers are required to figure out how much in taxes they owe under the traditional tax code, and then calculate what they owe under the AMT—and then pay the higher figure.

The problem with the AMT is that while it was designed to snare wealthy tax avoiders, it's poised to begin attacking the masses in coming years. An estimated 30 million taxpayers in 2010 could get trapped by the AMT, up from an estimated 3 million in 2004. That's because of the way the AMT was structured in its early days. It wasn't automatically indexed to inflation, so every year as incomes grow higher, the AMT sucks in more and more families. The AMT devilishly destroys many tax credits widely used by middle-class families, including deductions for state and local taxes as well as the exemptions for children that parents claim on their tax returns.

The AMT grew out of a 1969 report to Congress in which the Treasury noted that exactly 155 individuals with incomes above $200,000 at the time (the equivalent of about $1.2 million in 2004) didn't pay taxes in 1966 because of various tax breaks, loopholes, and tax shelters. Outraged lawmakers rushed to find a Band-Aid—the AMT. That Band-Aid hasn't been removed for decades, and beneath it now festers an entirely different sore.

In 2004 the AMT primarily affected taxpayers with incomes of between $100,000 and $500,000, particularly those in high-tax states like New York, California, New Jersey, and Massachusetts. But unless Congress reforms the way the AMT works, families with three or more kids will soon be in the grip of the AMT.

The irony in all of this is that the Treasury reported for 2001 that 3,385 taxpayers with incomes above $200,000 still paid no income taxes.

for your job, save all your receipts because you may be able to write off a large chunk of the cost. The list is long.

But if, as with many taxpayers, you're looking for those year-in and year-out tax savings, start with your employer's retirement savings plan or other retirement accounts. For every dollar you save up to the federal limit for the type of account you open, you'll reduce your taxes. You may remember this from the Planning chapter, but it's worth repeating here: If you save $10,000 in a 401(k), for instance, and you're in the 28% tax bracket, you'll reduce your taxes by $2,800. So fund your 401(k) until it hurts. Not only will you save on taxes, you'll be improving your future in retirement as well. Two benefits for the price of one.

In the same vein, fund a deductible IRA to the degree you're eligible. Again, you'll reduce your tax burden. You can fund an IRA for the previous year right up to the tax filing deadline on April 15. So if you want to save on this year's taxes, for instance, you can stash cash in an IRA as late as next April 15. If you know it will be difficult to come up with a lump of money at that exact time, then fund the account throughout the year, investing a set dollar amount every month or quarter. This offers a three-for-one benefit: tax savings, retirement planning, dollar-cost averaging—a tic-tac-toe of personal finance.

Establishing other pre-tax accounts with your employer also reduces taxes. Since taxes are such a headache, start deducting the medicine to fight them off.

Many employers offer so-called flexible spending accounts that pull pre-tax dollars from your paycheck and put them in an account that you can use to pay for items such as medical bills—including nonprescription drugs—and child care expenses. You can even use a particular flex spending account, a Transportation Management Account, to pay for your commute into the office every day. The pre-tax dollars you put into this account can pay for qualified parking (on or near bus premises), van pooling, and transit passes, fare cards, tokens, and vouchers used for mass transit such as trains, subways, light rail, ferries, and buses.

As with a 401(k) or other work-based retirement savings plan, the dollars you put into a flexible spending account are pre-tax, lowering your ultimate tax bill.

The caveat: You must use all the money in a flexible spending account each year or lose it. If you opt to save $2,400 a year, or $200 a month, in a medical spending account but by December you've spent only $1,000 . . . well, you had better go wild buying a stash of over-the-counter drugs or hit up your dentist and physician for checkups before the year ends. Otherwise, you lose whatever remains in the account.

The flip side: If in January you fall while disco dancing on roller skates and break your wrist, and the doctor bills not covered by insurance are $750, you can bill your account for those out-of-pocket expenses and it will pay the full cost. Even though you have only $200 in the account at that point, federal guidelines recognize that major maladies don't wait to arise until your account is fully funded in December. As such, the law allows the plan to cover, at any point during the year, up to the total amount you've pledged to put into the account.

How much money you withhold from your paycheck offers another opportunity to save on taxes. As noted earlier, overwithholding doesn't make sense because you're effectively giving the government control over your money for a year, and you're getting nothing for it. Ideally, you want to *owe* the IRS a negligible sum each year. That shows you retained control of all your own money and a tiny sliver of the government's.

By withholding properly, the amount of taxes pulled from your paycheck will shrink. You're not actually *saving* on your taxes with this strategy since this is money you don't owe Uncle Sam to begin with. Nevertheless, your paycheck increases, allowing you to use your money for your own wants during the year.

Be careful, though. You don't want to underwithhold. If at tax time you ultimately owe the IRS more than 10% of your total tax bill for the year, you might have to pay an interest penalty for not paying enough into the system along the way. As mentioned earlier, the Web sites www.PaycheckCity.com and www.IRS.gov both offer calculators to help you determine the proper amount to withhold.

THE AUDIT

Old joke: Why do sharks not attack tax auditors?

Professional courtesy.

Aside from having to file for bankruptcy, no other personal finance incident causes more angst than learning you're the subject of an IRS tax audit. The mental image of a government tax auditor ripping apart every decimal point on your tax return and demanding a single receipt for a business trip to Kankakee three years ago sends taxpayers into paroxysms. Of course, that might be more media hype than fact, but no matter.

The truth is, many audits are cursory. The IRS doesn't have the resources to scrutinize the accuracy of most returns. For that reason U.S. taxpayers are largely on the honor system when it comes to paying their fair share to keep the country running. Still, just to keep taxpayers as honest as possible, the agency conducts random audits each year, meaning that law-abiding taxpayers are sometimes scooped up in the net.

In some cases an audit can be as simple as the IRS informing you via letter that some entry on your tax return doesn't jibe—a correspondence audit. The agency typically tells you what you need to submit or asks you to provide some sort of proof or clarification. Photocopy the proof, enclose a polite letter explaining your position, and that may be all there is to it. The IRS goes away. No Rottweiler of an auditor shows up at your door looking to take a bite out of your wealth. You don't have to hire a tax attorney, and you owe no additional money.

Then again, a tax audit can make a proctology exam seem like a warm bath, particularly if your tax return is larded with red flags. In such a case the audit can be excruciatingly detailed.

What might pique the agency's interest? A few red flags include taking a home-office deduction since it is often claimed in error; excessive charitable donations; consistent losses reported on a home business; omitting income that the IRS knows about from other sources; excessive itemized deductions; high-income earners; dubious tax shelters.

If you are selected for an audit, don't panic. Instead, prepare:

- Know your rights. IRS Publication 1, *Your Rights as a Taxpayer,* details those rights. You can find that publication online at www.irs.gov/publications/p1/index.html.

- Know your position: Research your particular issue in IRS publications and commercial tax guides to make sure that your deduction has a basis you can defend.

- Organize receipts, canceled checks, credit-card bills, or whatever you based your deduction on, and bring them with you. Don't show up with a shoebox full of disheveled papers and crumpled receipts; it leaves the impression that your return might not be very accurate.

- Rebuild missing records. If you find that you're missing necessary documents, reconstruct them as best you can.

- Request more time. If you need more time to build your proof or to consult a tax attorney, ask for it. The IRS is generally pretty accommodating.

- Don't use prior year returns as proof. Tempting as it might be to use a previous return, if an auditor sees something in that return that looks questionable, that return could be next in line for an audit.

- Use a tax pro. For any inquiry other than the most basic issues that you can address and prove on your own, it's best to use a tax professional who knows the intricacy of the tax code and can better defend your deductions.

- Lose the attitude. Do you respond well when people you don't know act like jerks to you? Why would an auditor respond any differently? No matter how angry or agitated you might be, remain cool.

- Don't lie. If you don't know the answer to a question or if you don't have the proper documentation, say you don't know and ask for time to find what you need or to research it. Don't try to wing it with some fabricated answer; the auditor is certain to believe you're hiding something.

- Negotiate effectively. Don't negotiate how much money you think the IRS should or shouldn't make you pay. Instead, negotiate the deduction itself, arguing its merits in terms of the tax issue involved.

- Go to court. If you don't agree with the auditor's final verdict, you can always appeal to the auditor's manager or go to tax court. The upside is that even if you lose, in many cases the amount of money you owe will be reduced. The downside is that the appeal can raise other issues that the auditor might have missed, and it means the meter keeps running on the interest that is accumulating on your tax bill.

How does the IRS pick its victims? Mostly through statistical analysis. The agency relies on something called the "discriminant function system," or DIF, to score returns based on a variety of factors. Like the formula for Coke, what goes into the DIF is a closely guarded secret, though tax pros say part of the recipe centers on anomalies. The IRS knows, for instance, how much taxpayers in a certain income range typically deduct for various items. If your return shows a pattern of items well beyond those ranges, your returns could be kicked aside for further review and possibly an audit.

ACKNOWLEDGMENTS

Writing a book seems like such a solitary process. Alas, it's not. While the author's name sits alone on the cover, the efforts of numerous people actually make the process of writing and publishing work. To that end I must thank several people for their help in making this book work.

Ken Wells and Roe D'Angelo at *The Wall Street Journal* shepherded my book proposal to the right people—those people being Annik LaFarge and John Mahaney, both at Crown Publishing. Annik, in particular, offered invaluable guidance throughout the writing process that helped this book come together quickly.

My bosses at the *Journal,* Edward Felsenthal and Bob Sabat, once again tolerated my writing a book when I could have instead been easing their daily worries about what personal finance story is going to be in the Personal Journal section the following morning. I thank you for your patience.

I must thank my colleague Ellen Schultz for sharing with me through the years her immeasurable expertise on insurance and annuities, much of which is reflected in these pages. Marilyn Cohen, at Envision Capital Management, in Los Angeles, shared an abundance of knowledge about the world of bonds; while Ed Slott, in Rockville Centre, New York, allowed me to tap into his expertise in IRAs. David Darst, at Morgan Stanley's headquarters in New York, has been an invaluable source through the years and helped ensure the accuracy of the section on investing. Tom Hohl, at Boston's Fidelity Investments, provided assistance with the intricacies of 401(k) retirement savings plans; while Kevin Kelso, at Farmers Insurance in Los Angeles, and Gary Tolman, at San Francisco–based Esurance.com, both provided insights into the insurance world. My friend Andrea Lindley undertook the task of proofreading this book, even though she claimed the subject matter "bored me to death"; and the city of Vancouver, British Columbia, provided me a beautiful spot in Stanley Park, where a great deal of this book came together on my laptop.

Finally, to my wife, Amy, and my two kids, Zachary and Nicole: Thank you each for putting up with Dad locking himself in the office every night for months. I love you all for your support, and I apologize for the movies and games I missed and the family time that was spent without me. One of these days I'll find a way to repay each of you. Now, about that next book I want to write . . .

INDEX

ABOUT THE AUTHOR

JEFF D. OPDYKE is a financial reporter who has covered investing and personal finance for *The Wall Street Journal* for the past twelve years. He is also a columnist for *The Wall Street Journal* Sunday supplement, writing the Love & Money column that is syndicated in roughly ninety papers nationwide and which explores the nexus of personal finance and personal relationships. Opdyke is the author of *Love & Money: The Life Guide to Financial Success*. Prior to joining the *Journal* in 1993, Opdyke was a staff writer for the *Orange County Register* in Southern California and the *Fort Worth* (Tex.) *Star-Telegram*. He spent a nine-month sabbatical as an analyst and trader for a Dallas-based hedge fund. Opdyke is a graduate of the Louisiana State University Manship School of Journalism. He lives in Baton Rouge, Louisiana, with his wife, Amy, and their two children.

A HIGHLY PRACTICAL, HANDS-ON APPROACH TO PERSONAL FINANCE

The Wall Street Journal.
Personal Finance Workbook
$13.95 paper (Canada: $21.00)
ISBN: 978-0-307-33601-9

The Wall Street Journal.
Complete Money and Investing Guidebook
$14.95 paper (Canada: $21.00)
ISBN: 978-0-307-23699-9

The Wall Street Journal.
Complete Identity Theft Guidebook
How to Protect Yourself from the Most Pervasive
Crime in America
$13.95 paper (Canada: $17.95)
ISBN: 978-0-307-33853-2

The Wall Street Journal.
Complete Retirement Guidebook
How to Plan It, Live It and Enjoy It
$14.95 paper (Canada: $19.95)
ISBN: 978-0-307-35099-2

The Wall Street Journal.
Guide to Starting Fresh
How to Leave Financial Hardships Behind and
Take Control of Your Financial Life
$15.00 paper (Canada: $17.00)
978-0-307-58873-9

The Wall Street Journal.
Complete Estate Planning Guidebook
$14.99 paper (Canada: $16.99)
978-0-307-46127-8

AVAILABLE FROM THREE RIVERS PRESS WHEREVER BOOKS ARE SOLD.